M000219120

Liberty Vs. Tyranny

Liberty Vs. Tyranny

By

Col. Andrew P. O'Meara, Jr.

with

Tony Moore

Briton Publishing LLC
1237 Glenwood Trail
Batavia, Ohio 45103
www.britonpublishing.com

ISBN 1-978-10879625-5-9 Hardback
ISBN 1-978-10879356-2-1 Paperback

www.britonpublishing.com

*To the brave Americans lost in
Vietnam as victims of fake news.*

Contents

LIST OF FIGURES

ABBREVIATIONS

AG: US Army Military Lawyers

ANTIFA: Marxist front originally formed to oppose Fascism (Italy) and National Socialism (Nazi Germany)

ARVN: Army of the Republic of Vietnam (South Vietnam)

BLM: Black Lives Matter

CCP: Chinese Communist Party

CIA: Central Intelligence Agency (US)

CP (USA): Communist Party of the USA

DOJ: Department of Justice (US)

DRV: Democratic Republic of Vietnam (North Vietnam)

GVN: Government of Vietnam (Saigon government)

IED: Improvised Explosive Device

KGB: Soviet Intelligence Agency

KMT: Nationalist Party (Republic of China)

NATO: North Atlantic Treaty Organization

NKVD: Soviet secret police

NLF: National Liberation Front

NOW: National Organization of Women

PAVN: People's Army of Vietnam (North Vietnam)

PLA: People's Liberation Army of Communist China

PRC: People's Republic of China

PRU: Provincial Reconnaissance Unit

PTSD: Post Traumatic Stress Disorder

RF/PF: Regional Forces/Popular Forces (RVN)

RVN: Republic of Vietnam (South Vietnam)

SDS: Students for a Democratic Society

SEATO: Southeast Asia Treaty Organization

SF: Special Forces (US)

UCMJ: Uniform Code of Military Justice (US)

VA: Department of Veteran's Affairs (US)

VC: Viet Cong

VCI: Viet Cong Infrastructure

VVAW: Vietnam Veterans Against the War

USSR: Soviet Union

FOREWORD

Two hundred and forty-four years after the founders signed the Declaration of Independence America is again facing a revolution. This time it is not English tyranny we are fighting. Instead of an English Redcoat army, we are facing domestic enemies who are determined to destroy our constitutional republic and dismember the free enterprise system. The domestic enemy consists of power-hungry extremists who are determined to seize power at any cost. At the 2020 Mount Rushmore celebration of Independence Day President Donald Trump declared the extremists a fascist, totalitarian movement dedicated to the overthrow of the republic established by the founders in 1776.

Faced with ongoing insurrection, Americans find themselves under relentless assaults in an undeclared civil war. Deep state resistance attacks the president and seeks to overthrow the government. They attack the administration fabricating offenses to investigate, while impeaching the president for conduct of lawful and

1

legitimate affairs of state. They pirate agencies of the administrative state (e.g., the IRS and DOJ) to sabotage political rivals and they weaponized the federal bureaucracy (e.g., the CIA, FBI and the NSC) to spy on the GOP and destroy their rivals.

The Left fights with premeditated intent to annihilate their opposition. Whereas the GOP seeks compromise, and the rule of law, Democrat leaders act to destroy anyone who stands in their way. They wage political warfare using character assassination to ruin reputations, fabricating crimes to imprison the innocent, and eliminating opponents, e.g., Brett Kavanaugh, Lieutenant General Mike Flynn, Vince Foster and many more.

They would replace free enterprise with failed utopian fantasies of unhinged philosophers, principally Karl Marx. Their declared purpose is to fundamentally transform America into a socialist police state. They use multiple strategies to seize power. They emulate Lenin's tactics to take down the government in a violent coup. At the same time, they employ Saul Alinsky's approach to take control of the administrative state by stealth and the ballot box using massive voter fraud. They have raised a motley army of brainwashed vandals to trigger an insurrection against individual liberty, the rich American heritage, the duty of self-reliance, and government by, for and of the people.

The rebels work at many levels to destroy the American dream and our way of life. Activist judges abuse their authority to hamstring the executive branch, while radical judges work to financially ruin and imprison GOP officials.

The mainstream media and social media work as partners of the Democratic National Committee (DNC) to spread propaganda to ruin Republicans, to applaud Democrats, and to conceal the criminal past of their revolutionary movement. Communist fronts conduct protests across the country to disarm Americans, abolish police departments, and empty prisons. Rioters tear down statues, burn our cities, and carry out a ruthless campaign to assassinate cops. It is an ugly picture that is intended to intimidate citizens and to impose socialism upon America.

Americans have watched as spoiled intellectuals have turned on taxpayers, who are their benefactors, betraying the noble principles of the founders. Radical professors have abused academic freedom to indoctrinate students with hatred of America. Their radicalized followers incite riots and terrorize entire communities. Their actions are illegal, unethical, and destructive. The time has come to take a stand against these disgraceful traitors.

- No more treason masquerading as academic freedom.
- No more racial hatred employed to exploit minorities.
- No more socialist class warfare waged against the people.
- No more radical identity politics to destroy national unity.
- No more mindless looting and burning of our communities.

Universities that have become bastions for sheltering communist insurrections must be rehabilitated or abolished. Their radical dons must be held accountable for treason. They have violated their sacred right to liberty by reason of their treasonous assaults upon our constitutional republic. Their endowments should be taken by state and federal governments to pay for high crimes against the American people committed by self-serving academic rebels.

They justify their revolution with accusations that America is a racist country. It is an outrageously false claim that savages the reputations of generous and law-abiding citizens. The leaders of their insurrection against "racism" are minorities, who have been elected by their fellow citizens to the highest positions of authority in the land. These shameless hypocrites who govern American cities, states and the federal government are living proof of the fallacy of their cause.

The claims of racism are made by minorities and their allies, including senators Chuck Schumer, Kamala Harris, Maxine Waters, Cory Booker, and congressional representatives such as Alexandra Ocasio Cortez and the Black Caucus. Their presence – as elected representatives of the people – proves America is not racist. In fact, a good case can be made that the USA is the least racist nation in history with the exception of the radical Left that makes no effort to hide their racial hatred.

This is the other side of the story of the socialist rebellion in America. The racial jihad of communist protesters is rooted in deception and fallacy. America is not racist. The true racists are those who play the race card to manipulate public opinion (e.g., silence is violence), prohibit free speech, shake down commercial businesses, inflame racial hatred, and destroy those targeted as enemies of the people. The true racists are Antifa, Black Lives Matter and radicals inciting riots, burning private property, and destroying American communities.

We are threatened, but the socialist uprising is not going anywhere. We have news for the radical insurgents. As John Paul Jones declared, "We have not yet begun to fight." American citizens have overcome many threats; although they have seldom seen anything to compare with the denunciations, brutality, and hatred exhibited by these shameless hypocrites. Despite their resistance, rebellion and sabotage Americans stand united against injustice, tyranny, and treason to preserve liberty and justice for all.

We do not stand alone in the battle for the American dream and our way of life. President Donald J. Trump has rallied patriotic Americans across the country to support his Make America Great Again agenda. His brilliant leadership has restored the economy and brought American industry and jobs back home to the USA. His defense of American sovereignty has protected national borders, halted globalist give-away programs, and broken-down trade barriers. The President has brought troops home from endless foreign wars that enrich corrupt lawmakers and foreign mercenaries. President Trump has begun the legal battles essential to punish deep state criminals, expose voter fraud scams, and restore the even-handed administration of our judicial system.

Conservative educators, farmers, steel workers, miners, religious groups, and patriotic citizens are united as never before against the ruthless attacks to overthrow the government. Loyal Americans like Andy O'Meara are showing the way by leadership at the grassroots level. *Liberty Vs Tyranny* is a primer on the methods of operations of communist insurgents. The chapters of Andy O'Meara's book were written as professional commentaries during a long career fighting communist insurgencies and terrorism.

Liberty Vs Tyranny is an important resource for Americans resisting communist revolutionaries. The book shows the organizational structure, the political strategy and the tactical methods used by Lenin, Mao, Ho Chi Minh and the American Communist Party (CPUSA). Law enforcement officers, military intelligence officers, FBI agents and concerned citizens can prepare themselves for the challenges we face opposing communist insurrections by lessons contained in *Liberty Vs Tyranny*.

Loyal Americans should read Andy O'Meara's accounts of the wars fought by earlier generations of Americans who battled communism in Europe, East Asia, the Middle East, and Latin America. It is a proud chapter in our national experience. Regrettably, it is a story that has been suppressed by socialist journalists and radical educators to mask their betrayal of America.

I wish to express my thanks to Andy O'Meara and his generation of American servicemen and women, who devoted their lives to fighting communism on many fronts. The lessons they learned through long and difficult service can guide us as we defend freedom and this great land we love.

Lt. Gen. Tom Mc Inerney (USAF Retired)
12/22/2020

INTRODUCTION

More than a century after Progressives began their revision of American education, our society is captured by their language, values, and philosophy. The new identity crafted for America by Progressive reformers has discredited American tradition, now seen as corrupt. The reformers, primarily educators, have altered all levels of education to impart politically correct norms and critical views of history.

The past has been recast by their narratives. Columbus has become an anti-hero. Courageous pioneers who have braved the wild frontier to open the West are recast as exploiters of Native Americans and spoilers of the environment. Brilliant innovators who built industry and modernized America are portrayed as oppressors of workers. A rich history of national achievements has been discredited in the process. The past that is still honored by Conservatives of my generation is seen by our children as corrupt.

While conservatives have been developing America and defending freedom, progressive reformers have introduced socialist doctrine into public schools and have recast America's past. Conservatives have taken exception to the trashing of the national heritage; however, they have been faced with enormous difficulties in restoring all that has been lost. Correcting the problem is a monumental task. Expunging socialist teachings and restoring our lost past entails restoring traditional history lessons and texts, while fundamentally reforming our educational system to eliminate un-American doctrine aimed at the overthrow of the government. It is a daunting challenge that appears beyond our reach. Fortunately, we are not alone.

The push back against revisionist history has been broadly based. Conservative journals and newspapers such as Commentary, The New Criterion, The Claremont Review of Books, The Epoch Times and The Washington Times have led the way. Private institutions of higher learning such as the Franciscan University of Steubenville and Hillsdale College have carried the torch to preserve the legacy of Western Civilization. Conservative think tanks such as The Heritage Foundation have challenged progressive socialist reforms through support of conservative authorities and funding assessments of the challenges posed by progressive reforms.

Traditional educators and dedicated journalists such as Samuel Blumenfeld and Alex Newman have exposed abuse of public education programs to abolish American heritage (*CRIMES OF THE EDUCATORS: HOW UTOPIANS ARE USING GOVERNMENT SCHOOLS TO DESTROY AMERICAN*

CHILDREN; 2014). Fox News and talk radio push back against the disinformation of the liberal media to present daily news untainted by the politically correct doctrine of progressive reformers.

Our survey of the work of progressive reformers builds upon the foundation laid by conservative periodicals, newspapers, colleges, think tanks and authors to define the impact of progressive doctrine upon our culture and society. Of interest in this review has been the impact of progressive reforms upon American institutions and foreign policy. While our survey primarily addresses the threats and accomplishments of my generation, the lessons learned have a wider application in identifying the uncompromising character of threats posed by present-day socialist challenges to our national interests.

The leitmotiv of our inquiry is a morality play that juxtaposes the motives of the agents of change of modern times.

Whereas the philosophers of the French enlightenment and their followers adopted atheism, their opponents have remained faithful to Western Civilization. Consequently, we find a dichotomy that persists between the roles played by the agents of change of east and West. Josef Stalin said it best. At their meeting in Yalta in 1944, Winston Churchill observed that God is on our side. Stalin replied the Devil is on our side. Stalin went on to observe that the Devil is a good communist.

This survey includes conflicts on the field of battle and on the Homefront. Often, details of battlefield events are difficult to find in contemporary literature (e.g., American successes in Vietnam). In retrospect, the facts appeared obvious to those of us involved in the actions. Real-world accounts that present serious challenges to existing teachings are frequently suppressed as heresy by institutional gatekeepers. (A famous example of denunciation of reality was the silencing of Galileo, a renowned enlightenment scholar, who was persecuted for his discoveries that appeared to contradict Biblical accounts of the universe.)

Concerning the need for the study of Liberty Vs. Tyranny, it contains insights that are common sense. They appear obvious once brought to the attention of impartial observers. The failure to identify the insights is attributed to a suspension of critical thinking that has restricted political philosophy during the era of Progressive reform. Politically correct gatekeepers have not allowed discussions that challenge socialist doctrine. The resulting group think has hindered the advancement of political philosophy.

In the period of suspended discussions, obvious questions went unasked and unanswered. The absence of discussion and analysis resulted in an era in which the development of the discipline was stunted. Thus, students of political philosophy have experienced a curtailment of learning that has impoverished inquiry and denied opportunities for original thinking to flourish.

The stagnation of the discipline among progressive educators is indicative of the pressing need to resume critical thinking throughout the academic community. We must resume critical thinking within progressive institutions of higher learning, or we must acknowledge the discipline has entered a period of decline like that experienced in the Soviet Union under Stalin or in the People's Republic of China (PRC) during the Greater Proletarian Cultural Revolution.

Whereas indoctrination requires conformity and group think, science and reason demand unfettered academic freedom and intellectual honesty. Inasmuch as the American constitutional order is predicated upon individual liberty, which presumes academic freedom, Americans must restore the independence of the academic community. Such independence requires the academic freedom to exercise reason as opposed to ideological conformity. Americans must restore academic freedom or fall victim to false gods and alien doctrines.

Before we progress any further, we need to ask why this quest for answers to the travesty of revisionist history that haunts American education? As we have observed, revisionist history has impoverished America by disparaging the past and denying the rich heritage of our people. Whereas the character of revisionist history in America has been addressed, the consequences for the author have been implicit. Inasmuch as political philosophy is not a matter of concern for the average veteran, a few words on the origins of this book are in order.

My initial service as an American adviser to the Vietnamese Army in 1962 convinced me that the American military and specifically Andy O'Meara did not understand the enemy. It also was evident the War was far from over. We would be fighting communist insurgencies for many years to come. I made up my mind to study wars of national liberation. I was determined to be better prepared to fight the Viet Cong when I returned to South Vietnam.

Over the next twenty years, I studied revolutionary warfare and political philosophy at every opportunity. (Political philosophy covers the doctrine and theory of Marxist revolutionary warfare.) I pursued graduate studies at military colleges and civilian universities. The studies provided the opportunity to recognize the methods, rational, and tactics of communist insurgents attacking American allies in Asia and Latin America.

Attendance at the Army Command and General Staff College, the Army War College and the National War College provided me with an appreciation of revolutionary warfare. Civilian universities allowed me to study the works of Karl Marx, V. I. Lenin and Mao Zedong while participating in graduate studies at the University of Wisconsin, Milwaukee (while teaching ROTC) and at the University of Munich, Federal Republic of Germany (FRG) as a student in the Foreign Area Officer Program.

Both the military colleges and the civilian universities offered unique opportunities, as well as occupational hazards. Both environments offered the chance to study the best and the brightest authorities of the day, while they simultaneously exposed students to the turbulent ideological conflicts of the day that took a toll among our comrades along the way.

Both worlds suffered from resistance to change. Whereas progressive academic institutions rejected challenges to socialist doctrine, the Army had a history of resistance to change. Despite its conservative outlook, the Army met the enormous challenge posed by multiple conflicts since I entered West Point in July 1955, soon after the end of hostilities in Korea.

Armies tend to prepare for the last war because the ordeal is still freshly implanted in our thinking. My initial tactical training at the Academy prepared me to serve as a company grade infantry officer in the Korean War. The Korean War had been especially bloody owing to the enemy reliance upon massive infantry night attacks of the units assigned to the US Eighth Army.

Mao used the Korean War to stabilize Chinese society in the wake of the Revolution by sending politically unreliable troops to be slaughtered by the Americans. The Chinese Communists took advantage of the Korean War to purge the People's Liberation Army (PLA) of politically unreliable soldiers who had changed sides following the defeat of the Nationalists in 1949.

The sacrifice of countless lives by the Chinese Communists was intentional and considered essential to help resolve political challenges experienced in building socialism in the People's Republic of China. It involved a massive human slaughter that contributed to the prolongation of the war, as well as to fraudulent claims of American use of biological warfare to cover-up the reasons for the massive casualties suffered by the PLA.

The massive Korean bloodletting left lasting impressions upon all concerned. Since the war, officers in the PLA have been great admirers of American artillery that did the lion's share of the killing. At the same time, coping with massive infantry night attacks was the focus of Army tactical instruction when I entered the Military Academy sixty-five years ago. It was ugly business. On countless occasions I have counted my blessings for a fate that allowed me to avoid the savage infantry fighting and the bitter cold of the Korean War. The chapters that follow are the fruit of efforts to address the many challenges faced during the military service of my generation – most especially revolutionary warfare. Many of the lessons learned are still relevant to the complex social environment that confronts contemporary American students and faculty.

Chapter 1:

THE WAR AGAINST THE WAR

Many years have passed since the march of antiwar protesters have created chaos in our streets and turned victory in Vietnam into defeat. In the intervening years, we have suppressed memories of our losses, while overlooking events that have turned our world upside down. Despite painful memories, it is important to look back. There are lessons to be learned from the hectic days of protest when the law has been openly violated with impunity.

The Vietnam War touched all Americans. It created a cultural upheaval that had left a chasm between and within generations. The legacy of the war still casts a shadow over the political landscape, revealing lasting differences between those who participated in the event of the period. To understand the transformation, we must examine the events that altered America to determine what it was about the war that had so antagonized our people.

Those of us serving in uniform did our duty under circumstances that were humiliating and unlawful. Protesters threw excrement at soldiers guarding the Pentagon. We had to step over inert bodies to get into the Pentagon. Recruiters were not permitted on campus at the best private colleges and universities in the country. Soldiers returning home were accused of being murderers. Draft board facilities were broken into and trashed. College facilities were bombed, and acts of sabotage were committed.

Intellectuals who led the antiwar movement were disaffected academic professors who rejected traditional American values. Their influence on their students galvanized protests that shaped public opinion. Their activities disrupted military recruiting and training.

One of the young leaders of the antiwar movement was John Kerry, a Yale graduate and former naval officer. Kerry served in the brown-water navy in the rivers and coastal waters of South Vietnam. After his brief four-month tour of duty in Vietnam, Kerry joined the protest movement as a member of the Vietnam Veterans Against the War. The group organized protests and investigated the conduct of the war. Their efforts produced charges of torture and war crimes. The investigation was conducted by people who had never served in Vietnam. Investigation of the charges by Naval Intelligence found the charges to be without merit.

Charges of War Crimes

The VVAW descended on Washington to conduct antiwar demonstrations that received extensive media coverage. On April 23, 1971, John Kerry appeared before the Senate Committee on Foreign Relations. In his televised testimony, Kerry repeated the VVAW claims of "crimes committed on a day-to-day basis with the full awareness of officers at all levels of command." He alleged war crimes were committed by the military "in a fashion reminiscent of Genghis Khan." [1] The televised testimony had a chilling impact on support for the war, while galvanizing support for the antiwar movement.

Where did America go wrong? What caused the attacks on American foreign policy? Was the role of John Kerry influenced by defiance of the administration that informed opinion on the Yale campus during the sixties? Did Kerry's undergraduate studies predetermine his actions? These questions call attention to events that transpired at Yale during the war that influenced American public opinion.

Yale University served as a leader in the antiestablishment thinking that challenged American foreign policy during the Cold War. William F. Buckley produced a telling study that identified anti-American trends at Yale as early as 1951. The study documented that socialism was taught in

---

[1] Who Is John Kerry? (Alexandria, VA: The American Conservative Union, 2004), pp. 49–57.

virtually all relevant courses offered by the university, making Yale a bastion of leftist thinking. [2]

The leftist leanings of the university were put to the test during the Cold War, when the United States took up containment of Soviet expansionism. Thereafter, an open breach between American foreign policy and the liberal academic community appeared to be only a matter of time. An uneasy modus vivendi between foreign policy makers and liberal intellectuals functioned during the early years of Kingman Brewster's tenure as president of the university. His support for American foreign policy collapsed during the Vietnam War, leading to Brewster's denunciation of the war and his leadership of opposition to the war in the academic community.

Mobilization of Student Protests

The breach followed measures taken by the Yale faculty to encourage student opposition to the war. Prominent faculty leaders promoting antiwar sentiment on the campus included philosophy professor Josiah Thompson, history professor Staughton Lynd, and university chaplain William Sloane Coffin Jr. All three were outspoken critics of the war who took their opposition into the classroom, politicizing instruction at the university.

---

[2] William F. Buckley Jr., God and Man at Yale (Washington: Regnery Publishing, Inc., 1986).

Thompson used a document written by student radicals entitled "Declaration of Conscience against the War in Vietnam" as a teaching vehicle for eliciting student declarations of conscience opposing the use of force in Vietnam. The exercise produced vocal student disapproval and mobilized opposition to the war on campus.

Advocating opposition to the war and questioning the legality of national policy, Lynd spoke at antiwar rallies on the Yale campus, as well as at the first large antiwar rally in Washington, DC. In 1965, Lynd joined Tom Hayden, founder of Students for a Democratic Society, and veteran communist Herbert Aptheker on a fact-finding mission to Hanoi in violation of the existing State Department ban on travel to North Vietnam. Speaking in Hanoi, Lynd accused President Johnson of lying and waging an immoral war.

University chaplain William Sloane Coffin Jr. organized the National emergency Committee of Clergy Concerned about Vietnam. Coffin used his position as university chaplain to challenge foreign policy. A fiery speaker, Coffin, likened the American government to the Nazis. Coffin declared Battell Chapel a sanctuary for opposition to the draft. He encouraged civil disobedience to discourage military presence on campus and prevent recruiting. He encouraged student protests in defiance of the draft.

Civil disobedience led to clashes between local authorities and student demonstrators. The Yale administration responded by taking steps to shield students from criminal prosecution. Under Brewster's direction, the university opposed FBI investigations of student involvement in demonstrations and civil disobedience. By creating a university sanctuary for antiwar activities, Brewster encouraged student opposition, including efforts to form a second front against the war, an objective of the Students for a Democratic Society.

An Immoral War

Yale became a center for opposition to the war, rallying college faculty members and clergy across the country to the antiwar cause. Brewster came out against the war at a rally of some fifty thousand protesters on the New Haven Green. Kingman Brewster closed the Yale ROTC program and declared the war immoral in October 1969. In so doing, he accused the men and women serving in Vietnam of being war criminals.

Brewster's actions vilified American servicemen and women with charges that would haunt them for years. [3] Meanwhile, faculty leaders of the antiwar movement made headlines that encouraged the spread of protests across the country.

Having opposed the war from the start, the liberal media bought into Brewster's denunciation that became the collective wisdom of the establishment. In the wake of

---

[3] Anthony Lewis, "A Thoughtful Answer to Hard Questions," New York Times (October 17, 1969).

Brewster's denunciation of the war, the American bishops of the Roman Catholic Church and the American Council of Churches declared the war immoral. Thereafter, Hollywood and television savaged the uniformed military as war criminals.

The escalation of the opposition to the war resulted in the closing of ROTC detachments and the loss of public support for the war. These were not insignificant consequences inasmuch as public opposition to the war resulted in congressional action to terminate American support for the Government of South Vietnam, causing the defeat of our allies in South Vietnam.

Having acted as the vanguard in mobilizing domestic opposition to the war, did Kingman Brewster and the Yale faculty bear responsibility for the outcome of their actions? Did individual faculty members who led the protests and mobilized the opposition to the war bear responsibility for their actions that led to the defeat of South Vietnam? And would John Kerry have turned against the war, leading the opposition to the war and joining the VVAW, had the Yale faculty not radicalized student opposition to the war?

John Kerry assumed a leading role in the antiwar movement after his discharge from active duty. John Kerry did not complete one campaign in Vietnam. His observations were limited in scope. And with his limited observations, he judged all Vietnam veterans to be war criminals. He filed no charges against men under his command for war crimes, even though he claimed they were responsible for carrying out atrocities. And he requested early release from combat for wounds that required no hospitalization. He wrote himself up for three awards of the Purple Heart, which he used as the basis for a request for early release from combat. Kerry's request took advantage of administrative measures intended to save men with multiple war wounds from more exposure to combat operations.

Did American servicemen commit atrocities as claimed by John Kerry? The answer is an emphatic no. Atrocities are war crimes that violated the rules of engagement observed by all troops in country. Whereas Americans prosecuted anyone accused of war crimes, the communists committed atrocities daily.

It was state policy of Hanoi to kill all members of the Saigon regime. Mass murder was a common occurrence. Especially brutal was the annihilation of Roman Catholic villages that were routinely destroyed with no prisoners taken.

Hanoi had a score to settle with Catholics. Entire Roman Catholic villages had fled the Red River Delta when the French pulled out of North Vietnam. They had been resettled in South Vietnam. Hanoi considered the Catholic villagers to be traitors. They fell into a category designated enemy of the people. They were marked for elimination. (It is a bitter irony that the Roman Catholic Bishops in America accused Catholic villagers defending their homes in South Vietnam of waging an immoral war.)

John Kerry was a junior naval officer with limited time in South Vietnam and no time spent with ground troops conducting combat operations. He was unfamiliar with the rules of engagement for control of artillery fire. Kerry's statements that the use of free-fire zones was a violation of the Law of Land Warfare was wrong. John Kerry has subsequently admitted that his charges and Senate testimony were over the top. The fact is they were not over the top. They were wrong.

Rules of Engagement

Villages, towns, and hamlets in the rural countryside were designated *No-fire Zones*. *Restricted fire Zones* consisted of regions of scattered rural hamlets. *Free-fire Zones* were unpopulated regions that consisted of virgin rain forests, mangrove swamps, or mountainous regions. The rules of engagement prohibited the use of artillery fire support in *No-fire Zones*. District chiefs could give clearance to fire in *Restricted fire Zones* after making certain that artillery fire requests would not result in harm to the civilian population. *Free-fire Zones* were uninhabited and typically used by the Vietcong to establish base camps. Vietcong or North Vietnamese combat units encountered in *Free-fire Zones* could be immediately engaged by South Vietnamese or American troop units without getting clearance to fire from the district chief.

They Got It Wrong

Kingman Bruster and the Yale faculty got it wrong. The bishops and the clergy got it wrong. The war was a response to an invasion of South Vietnam by North Vietnam. It was not immoral. The war criminals were the North Vietnamese, and those who supported them. The South Vietnamese people trusted America, and we repaid them with false accusations of waging immoral warfare by misinformed bishops and clergy whose chilling denunciations isolated and abandoned the South Vietnamese people to their fate at the hands of ruthless communist invaders.

John Kerry's charges of genocidal warfare were wrong. His charges branded men and women innocent of wrongdoing as war criminals. Kerry's testimony before Congress turned many Americans against the war. Adverse public opinion resulted in termination of US support for the Government of South Vietnam by Congress. The unilateral abandonment of our allies amounted to capitulation by America that resulted in the defeat of our allies in South Vietnam.

In view of the evidence of John Kerry's false testimony, who is responsible? Actions have consequences. Those responsible for the actions are responsible for the consequences. The array of antiwar activists who have opposed the US war in Vietnam is extensive. They each bear responsibility for their actions. Those who have mobilized the opposition to the war bear a heavy burden of responsibility.

Acting together, opponents to the war spiked our cannon on the home front, while providing aid and comfort to North Vietnam. Their actions prolonged the war inasmuch as Hanoi extended the war in response to protests on the American home front, which gave North Vietnam reason to believe a continuation of the war would lead to final victory.

The antiwar movement must answer for the lives of troops who died during the extended campaigns launched by North Vietnam. They must answer for the soldiers who died fighting without artillery or air support as their country was torn apart by the massive attacks of the People's Army of Vietnam in 1975.

Kingman Brewster and the Yale faculty were responsible for actions that resulted in the fall of South Vietnam, banishing the people of South Vietnam to a life of servitude under a brutal communist regime. They must answer for the Vietnamese people who died in gulags and in leaky fishing boats at sea.

The veterans, who returned home to find they were despised by former friends and neighbors, never made the adjustment to being cast into the role of war criminals. They thought they were entitled to the respect their fathers enjoyed following WW II. Many took their own lives, victims of virtue signaling by students and faculty, as well as bishops and clergy, who sought recognition as followers of a "higher cause." It was the cause of Hanoi and the savage peasant armies they unleashed upon the people of South Vietnam.

The next time university dons and clergy launch a campus crusade against the USA, they need to ascertain the facts about who have attacked whom before they march through the streets. Learning the rules of engagement would also be helpful to avoid making false charges before Congress detrimental to American national interests and disgracing the men and women faithfully serving their country.

Chapter 2

<u>BETRAYAL BY THE FREE PRESS</u>

Ken Burns has captured an American era in a remarkable way. Working with his coproducer Lynn Novick, Ken Burns has produced a moving television documentary on the Vietnam War. The series records the testimonials of the academic community, Hollywood, and the news media. It faithfully presents the sights and sounds of the popular movement that opposed the war.

Prof. Robert F. Turner of the University of Virginia has written a review of the series that has appeared in *Vietnam Veterans for Factual History* magazine. Professor Turner challenges the documentary. He documents the events of the war as recorded in the official history of North Vietnam and the Pentagon Papers. Turner shows the documentary distorts the record. The documentary denies the invasions of South Vietnam by the North. It misrepresents the role of the Communist Party. It conceals Hanoi's responsibility for the National Liberation Front (NLF). Finally, it misrepresents the American involvement in the war.

What Burns and Novick get right is the narrative captures the conflict as reported by war correspondents and the news media—a significant achievement. Regrettably, the coverage of the war misinformed the public. The mainstream media covered up Hanoi's aggression and the leading role of the Communist Party in the Vietnam War.

The mainstream media adopted Hanoi's line, claiming the Americans and the Republic of South Vietnam were illegitimate and waging an immoral war. They claimed the South Vietnamese regime was corrupt and the American strategy violated the Geneva Conventions. Gaslighting Americans for over a decade by journalists destroyed public confidence, resulting in American capitulation followed by the defeat of the Saigon government.

Where did we go wrong? Why did the news media oppose the war? Unlike World War I and World War II, when Americans united in support of the war effort, the liberal establishment broke with national policy during the Vietnam War. National leadership in Congress and the State Department supported a foreign policy resisting Soviet expansionism. American policy opposed communist insurgencies. It was a foreign policy that challenged the leadership of the Soviet Union, communist insurgencies, and the liberal establishment in America.

As the Vietnam War escalated, antiwar literature clashed with the views of American policy makers. The clash of traditional values with support for the National Liberation Front brought the war home in a way few had experienced. Colleges, newsrooms, Hollywood studios, and main streets across the country became scenes of conflict as clashing values fractured public opinion.

Confronted by the liberal establishment, American foreign policy makers were forced to take their case to the American people. The reaction from the liberal establishment was swift, rejecting the official position with an outpouring of hostile accounts of the war. Liberal editors dug in their heels, instructing journalists to find the dirt on the American military. The liberal media reported the war as seen in Moscow and Hanoi rather than as seen in Saigon and Washington.

What does the Ken Burns documentary tell us? The Vietnam documentary reveals how the antiwar movement won the cultural war by dominating the popular culture. It was a significant victory, but not for the USA. Public support for the war effort withered under growing pressures of the Left that included antiwar films, protest ballads, hostile television reporting, revisionist literature, and critical newspaper accounts of the war.

Opposition to the war was encouraged on college campuses. Protests were organized by faculty members who staged teach-ins and demonstrations against the war. Protest marches were staged to mobilize opposition to the war. Members of the military were encouraged to desert. Confrontational protests escalated into violent demonstrations. Draft records were destroyed. Acts of sabotage and mutiny were recorded.

Hollywood celebrities organized publicity drives opposing the war. One Hollywood star assembled a traveling road show to protest what she called an *immoral war*. A cast of popular singers and musicians performed antiwar ballads. The show, called F**k the Army, performed outside army camps and stations, where soldiers got the message— *desert or become a war criminal*.

Activists opened coffeehouses that distributed drugs and antiwar literature. Coffeehouses sprang up in West Germany and America. They called on the troops to go AWOL. Young soldiers made easy targets. Thousands of soldiers accepted the antiwar message. They deserted, fleeing to sanctuaries in Canada and Sweden. Their lives suffered permanent disgrace when they were arrested, jailed, and dishonorably discharged for desertion.

Communist Party members (CPUSA) and Hollywood celebrities made trips abroad to mobilize opposition to the American role in the war. They visited Moscow, Havana, and Hanoi to show support for North Vietnam. Hollywood stars denied mistreatment of American POWs held by North Vietnam. Even worse, American airmen were denounced as war criminals.

A photograph of Jane Fonda manning an antiaircraft artillery piece with North Vietnamese gunners appeared in newspapers around the world. Years later, Fonda dismissed deep resentment over her conduct as a misunderstanding.

A misunderstanding? Support for the enemy in time of war amounted to betrayal of fellow countrymen in combat. It was a pattern of aid for the enemy that was common among college faculty and demonstrators who polarized public opinion and demonized the military. Nothing to fret about over a misunderstanding. Right? Guess again.

Young soldiers ended up as felons when they were conned into desertion. The tragedy escalated as families were crushed when sons and daughters were jailed and dishonorably discharged. More difficulties followed as the anger incited against the military triggered vilification of veterans as baby killers. Lives were devastated. Many took their own lives.

What baffled veterans was why antiwar leaders like Jane Fonda were never held accountable for betraying their country. Encouraging desertion was open support for the enemy that adversely affected American men and women serving in combat. Actions have consequences. Those responsible for the actions are also responsible for the consequences. Antiwar radicals committed treason. They should have been charged with treason. The Justice Department (DOJ) failed to hold traitors responsible for their crimes. The law was violated with impunity. Treason went unpunished—a rejection of the rule of law. Failure to uphold the law convinced the Left that they were above the law.

Thanks to Ken Burns, we are reminded of the persecution of America's sons and daughters during the Vietnam War. He reminds us that we have traitors and collaborators among us who have never been punished for their crimes.

It is a travesty that has allowed criminals to go scot-free. This travesty has corrupted the rule of law and damaged the integrity of the political system. It is an injustice that violates the fundamental principles of our legal system.

This injustice allows the Left to flaunt the law. It continues because the Department of Justice has failed to enforce the law. We must clean house or see the last best hope of man ruined by deep state criminals. The Pledge of Allegiance proclaims a falsehood until liberty and justice for all once again prevails in America.

Chapter 3:

MILITARY INSTITUTIONS AND THE POLITICAL CULTURE[4]

During the Cold War, the liberal media accused the Pentagon of forming a military-industrial complex. The story originated in the academic community and echoed communist propaganda. [5] The narrative held that American military strategy was the work of general officers who had vested interests in the armaments industry. The narrative accused the US military of writing a national strategy that

---

[4] This article first appeared in print as **Strategy and the Military Professional**, in two parts, in the January and February 1980 editions of Military Review, and the publication of the U.S. Army Command and General Staff College. The article was written by the author while studying as a graduate student (FAO Candidate) under Professor Doctor Peter Christian Lutz at the University of Munich, FRG in 1974.

[5] The narrative repeated remarks by President Eisenhower objecting to the hiring of former servicemen by the armaments industry as a conflict of interest. Eisenhower's naive words appeared to validate the Marxist doctrine.

enriched themselves and menaced "peace loving" communist countries.

Conservatives rejected the military-industrial complex story as fake news that echoed communist propaganda. American statesmen saw the US national strategy as a defensive response to Soviet policies exporting communism using military force. The US statesmen spoke with more than a little authority. They and their predecessors had written the US deterrence strategy. Despite the rejection of the Military- Industrial Complex narrative by Conservatives, it was widely accepted within the academic community.

The military-industrial complex narrative placed the blame for Cold War tensions squarely on the US military. Moreover, the narrative blamed the Pentagon for the strategy that caused the Vietnam War, thereby absolving North Vietnam of responsibility for starting the war by their invasion of South Vietnam. The narrative asserted that military professionals were the authors of the US national strategy—an assertion that was untrue.

Who Makes the National Strategy?

The character of strategy making was obvious to those who served with me in the Pentagon. Following my second tour of duty in Vietnam, I was assigned as an analyst in the Office of the Army Deputy Chief of Staff. As my first assignment, I was told to prepare distribution plans for anti-tank weapon systems. The Army budget request had contained requests for two new anti-tank weapons, the

Dragon and the TOW (TOW – tube launched, optically tracked, wire guided anti-tank system).

After weeks of analysis, I awaited a call to brief the plans to the Deputy Chief of Staff. The optimum plan assumed Congress approved the purchase of both anti-tank weapon systems. The second plan assumed Congress authorized procurement of only the TOW. The remaining plan assumed Congress authorized procurement of the Dragon, but not the TOW.

When the budget was eventually approved, my boss entered my office and announced the verdict saying, "Andy, you can stand down now. Congress didn't authorize procurement of any anti-tank weapons for the Army." My heart sank as I realized the implications of the decision. Congress had decided the Army would fight the next war without modern anti-tank weapons.

The Army would fight the next war, as we had fought World War II and the Korean War, when American infantrymen lacked weapons capable of destroying German Tiger Tanks and Soviet T-34 tanks. It was a shortsighted policy that was later reversed, but not in time for the infantrymen of my generation serving in Vietnam.

The Army was left with no alternative except to put a good face on a bad situation; i.e., American infantrymen would continue to fight at a disadvantage in close combat. Friendly close air support or artillery fire would be required to defeat enemy armor in close combat (responses that require suitable weather conditions or the presence of an artillery forward observer and artillery fire support at the point of enemy contact).

The experience clearly demonstrated who makes US national strategy. Whereas the Pentagon makes recommendations to Congress, the fate of the US armed forces is determined by elected representatives of the people who declare war and determine US national strategy. Congress determines when and where we fight, as well as the strength of the armed forces, the weapon systems we employ in combat, and the soldiers' pay. US general officers have no authority to make these decisions. Generals in the US armed forces do as they are told by the President to carry out the national strategy approved by Congress.

Despite the recognition of the harsh reality that prevailed by those serving on the Army General Staff, fantasies of general officers wielding vast powers was the prevailing wisdom of the liberal media and academe. After all, Marx and Lenin had predicted criminal behavior by capitalists; and it served the larger purpose of the liberal establishment that was determined to hold the US military responsible for the Vietnam War. They worked their will upon a naïve public that continues to believe in the incorrect Military-Industrial Complex narrative.

Their successful manipulation of public opinion distorted reality. Moreover, it exonerated the liberal establishment of betrayal of the USA, while it condemned my generation of warriors as war criminals.

Traditional definitions of "strategy" lend credence to the idea of general officers as the authors of military strategy. The English historian B. H. Liddell Hart defined "strategy" as the art of the general. Such thinking confused the role of warrior kings with the roles of subordinate general officers.

It was the king who marshaled the resources of the state to wage war and employed generals to train and lead the armed forces. The king directed the use of national resources, which formulated the national strategy. Contemporary political philosophers agree. They recognize that the allocation of scarce national resources is the essential function of strategy making.

National strategy making is a political act that exercises the highest authority in the state. It is a shared responsibility. The character of power-sharing is a function of the character of the political system. Alliances formed to acquire political power reflect the unique character of the state and its political system (e.g., the decision to employ military or police power to acquire power results in an authoritarian political system).

Allocation of resources is a decision made by political leaders that determines the strategy in a constitutional republic. In our republic it is a shared power carried out by Congress and the chief executive. As the elected representatives of the people, they allocate scarce resources to reflect the will of the people as mandated by campaign promises. The actions of elected representatives according to the will of the people reflect power-sharing by the people.

The importance of acting according to the will of the people in a constitutional republic cannot be overstated. Donald J. Trump would never have been elected president had GOP representatives followed the will of the people. Ignoring the electorate and their campaign promises Republicans ignited a grass roots rebellion. When American politicians ignore campaign promises, the people are denied their constitutional role in self-rule.

Rejecting the will of the people in a constitutional republic disenfranchises the electorate and signals the transition of the political system from republic to dictatorship. Consequently, ignoring the will of the people constitutes the assumption of dictatorial powers in a constitutional republic. It is a high crime against the Constitution and the republic.

The Role of the Military

The Constitutional Republic: In the USA, the military does not make the national strategy. General officers in the US Armed Forces carry out their oath of office to support and defend the Constitution and to carry out the orders of those appointed over them. If they don't make the strategy, what do American generals do? They carry out the national strategy, which includes implementing the national strategy, training armies, and leading in battle.

On occasion, generals go astray when the hubris of prestige results in actions that exceed their authority, as Gen. Douglas MacArthur did in Korea. Pres. Harry S. Truman sacked General MacArthur for insubordination. General MacArthur wanted to employ nuclear weapons to force the unconditional surrender of the Chinese Communists and North Koreans. It was a course of action that entailed risks of expanding the war, a UN peacekeeping mission.

The United States couldn't radically alter the strategy of the UN peacekeeping force without authorization by the UN Security Council—an unlikely outcome inasmuch as the Soviet Union had veto power. MacArthur's sin was he took his case to Congress, publicly advocating the revision of the UN strategy to permit the use of nuclear weapons, thereby exceeding his authority. MacArthur lost sight of who was in charge, a mistake that cost him his job.

If generals don't make strategy in the USA, do they make strategy in other political systems? The answer is yes. Generals make strategy in political systems that use internal security forces and the military to exercise political power—authoritarian and totalitarian dictatorships. [6]

---

[6] For a detailed discussion of authoritarian dictatorships see Samuel P. Huntington, Political Order in Changing Societies (The Colonial Press Inc.: 1968). For a detailed discussion of totalitarian dictatorships see Jeane J. Kirkpatrick, Dictators and Double Standards (Simon and Shuster Publishers:1982).

The Totalitarian (Communist) Dictatorship: Known as the dictatorship of the proletariat, it is government by the Communist Party in the name of the workers, the proletariat. Communist control of all activities in the society results in the label of totalitarian government. Inasmuch as the workers owned nothing and the Communist Party elite, or nomenclature controlled everything, the dictatorship was actually the dictatorship of the nomenklatura.

Communist revolutionaries use military forces to seize political power. Communist leaders employ military and police power to mobilize society and to take possession of industry, farming, and privately owned property. The military acted with Lenin and Mao in the power seizure and control of the state.

Communist revolutionaries use military forces to seize political power. Communist leaders employ military and police power to mobilize society and to take possession of industry, farming, and privately owned property.

The military acted with Lenin and Mao in the power seizure and control of the state. The military shared power inasmuch as general officers and KGB leaders sat on the politburo in the former Soviet Union. In the People's Republic of China general officers and party officials sat in the Party Congress thereby allowing the military to contribute to strategic planning and the allocation of resources.

The Authoritarian (Military) Dictatorship; military dictators use military force to seize control of the government. Military dictators like Franco in Spain and Pinochet in Chili act in the name of the people to defend the constitution or the republic. They do not attempt to alter the social structure but allow the people to retain their property and exercise personal freedom, when it poses no threat to the regime.

Franco and Pinochet prevented communist take-overs. In so doing they prevented the bloody purges of property owners, although over seven thousand clergy were murdered in Spain during the civil war. The governments of both Spain and Chili eventually reverted to civilian control. Pinochet supervised national elections that resulted in the return of the Chilean government to civilian control.

The people and the military act as partners in the power-sharing relationship in an authoritarian dictatorship. The military share power and protect the state. As such, the military exercise control of the society and contribute to strategy making in authoritarian dictatorships.

The Military Reflect the Civic Culture

How are we to understand the complex picture we have painted of the military in differing cultures – liberal societies as well as authoritarian dictatorships?

As participants in the social order, soldiers share the fate of the larger society that yields rewards and consequences. The soldier who serves as a guardian of liberal Western cultures has the privilege of transition from a lower to a higher degree of perfection, completion and fulfillment (William Durant's definition of happiness) simply by his or her participation in a rich and noble culture. On the other hand, savage nomads who accompanied Tamerlane on his campaigns of conquest in Central Asia shared the illiteracy, brutality and banality of a life of conquest, killing and plunder. The nobler calling of the liberal society yielded far greater rewards.

As members of a larger society, soldiers share the fate of their society. The rewards or consequences vary enormously as a function of the ends one serves. If one is born a Mongolian nomad, the chance to serve under the command of Tamerlane was a once in a life- time opportunity. Participation in his savage campaigns of conquest produced the barbaric character of a savage murderer. Similarly, the Nazi SS concentration camp guards who starved, murdered and burned the bodies of enemies of the Third German Reich shared the ignoble, criminal and soul-scaring experience of genocide.

How should we characterize the military in the three different political systems we have addressed? Military institutions mirror the character of the political system of the state. Whereas the United States Armed Forces reflect our democratic institutions dedicated to equality and liberty established in the Declaration of Independence, their counterparts in authoritarian dictatorships reflect the criminal acts of regimes dedicated to the annihilation of political enemies, parties and/or social classes.

The demeanor of soldiers reflects the deeds they perform. If required to carry out savage deeds, the soldiers will act accordingly. Consequently, the soldiers of the Red Army conducted themselves in the barbaric manner they carried out their extermination missions that amounted to genocide. Accordingly, the secret police and armed forces of murderous regimes have depraved brutal characters. It is not a matter of choice. It simply reflects that we are what we do.

The nature of national military institutions reflects their origins. American soldiers take an oath to defend the Constitution and obey the orders of those in authority over them. American armed forces were created by the American founding fathers. The authorization for the U.S. Army is found in the Constitution. The other American military services were created by acts of Congress. American armed forces are prohibited by law from carrying out police functions. Regulations prohibit American soldiers from participating in partisan political activities.

Whereas the armed forces of constitutional republics are established by their civilian founders, the military forces of authoritarian dictatorships often have origins that predate the revolution that brought the regime to power. The Bolsheviks relied upon deserters from the Tsarist Army, the military Garrison of Saint Petersburg and sailors of the Baltic fleet to carry out the coup, the October Revolution, that destroyed the Kerensky Regime.

The prior existence of collaborating military forces employed by Lenin in the power seizure had implications as far as the character of the new political system was concerned. The party leadership had formed an alliance with their revolutionary allies that granted a privileged position to the leadership of the military and secret police in the new socialist order. In return for their loyalty during the revolution and the civil war, the senior leaders of the military and secret police were treated as members of the nomenklatura. The functions of the leaders of the military and secret police included participation in the crimes of the revolutionary regime, as well as serving as partners in the Soviet governing establishment.

The Venn diagram shown in Figure 1 displays three different political systems that are formed by power-sharing by the people, political leaders and the military. The character of the military and internal security forces of the three political systems are dramatically different.

Whereas the Red Army and internal security forces of the Soviet Union liquidated those identified as enemies of the state, the military of constitutional republics function as guardians of the constitution. In the former case, the military and secret police liquidated the Kerensky regime and capitalists, both of which were crimes against humanity, whereas the military of liberal societies function as guardians of the people and their constitutional order.

The soldiers of military dictatorships tend to be conflicted as both guardians of the constitution, as well as brutal killers in purges to eliminate the revolutionaries. Thus, the character of the military and internal security forces of the three political systems are dramatically different. They range in character from brutal murderers to guardians of freedom, i.e., Nazi SS battle groups and NKVD executioners as opposed to law-abiding American citizens serving in uniform under civilian control.

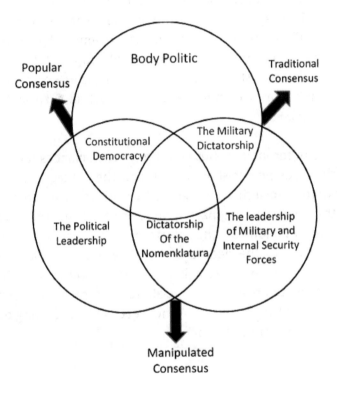

Figure 1: The Triad of Strategic Partnerships

Political Character of the Civic Culture

Alternative power-sharing partnerships are shown in Figure 1. The people and their elected representatives share power in a constitutional republic such as the American republic, labeled a constitutional democracy in Figure 1. The people and the military share power in military dictatorships such as Franco's regime in Spain. The Communist Party and internal security forces (KGB and armed forces) share power in a dictatorship of the nomenklatura or communist political system such as the former USSR.[7]

Three different societies result from the alliances formed by the three power-sharing partners. The character of the alternative societies is reflected by the consensus formed by the power-sharing pair. A popular consensus reflecting popular opinion of the electorate is formed by the partnership of the people and their elected officials in a constitutional republic. It is a power-sharing partnership that relies upon elected officials to perform their sworn duties to faithfully represent the electorate by carrying out their mandate from the people.

---

[7] Figure 1 shows the dictatorship of the proletariat as the dictatorship of the nomenklatura (Communist Party officials) since the nomenklatura administered the USSR, not the workers as called for by the Marxist doctrine.

In a constitutional republic, the character of the political system is dramatically changed when elected officials ignore their mandate from the people; inasmuch as the people no longer share in the power-sharing partnership. By elected officials ignoring their mandate, the people are no longer sovereign; and the state is governed by dictatorial power. The disenfranchisement of the people transforms the popular consensus into a manipulated consensus.

A Constitutional crisis is created by disenfranchisement of the people in a constitutional republic that demands revolutionary change, as occurred when Donald J. Trump was elected president. The electorate rejected the GOP establishment thereby altering the character of the Party and returning sovereignty to the people. Politicians, who went into business for themselves, had ignored their promises to the electorate abusing their public office for financial gain, causing a Constitutional crisis. The never-Trump members of the GOP establishment are the remnant of the rogue politicians, who attempted to subvert the government by altering the fundamental character of the Republic.

The manipulated consensus of the dictatorship of the nomenklatura reflects the character of the Communist Party that employs military and internal security forces to rule. Whereas the American people tell their civilian representatives how to think and manage their responsibilities; the Communist Party tells the captive population what and how to think. The power-sharing partnership reflects the authoritarian character of a political system that systematically manipulates public opinion to achieve the character of the new socialist man.

The traditional consensus formed by power-sharing by the people and the military allows the national identity of the people to be retained. The military dictator acts to defend the constitutional order from being overthrown by hostile groups. Thus, the military dictator serves the people—the body politic—by preserving the traditional political culture with their traditional consensus from revolutionary change as occurred in Spain under Franco and in Chili under Pinochet.

Viewed as an analytical tool, the Venn diagram shown in Figure 1 allows us to see contrasts between civic cultures that employ military resources in different ways to achieve very different ends. It tells us nothing about the social contract in the different societies shown. Consequently, it is of limited value. Nevertheless, to the extent that it allows us to recognize the dramatic differences between the military professions in vastly different civic cultures, it is worthy of our consideration.

The military in a liberal society governed by a constitutional order has an entirely different character than that demonstrated by the military in societies that employ military force for political ends within the domestic society.

Examples of power-sharing partnerships are depicted in figure 2. Figure A represents a power-sharing partnership in which the partners are equal or the same. At the time of the First World War, the German political system was composed of the military sharing power with the Kaiser on behalf of the people in a monarchy. Given the requirement for universal military service and the franchise limiting the vote to adult male property owners, the partners were very nearly identical.

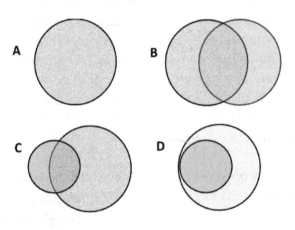

Figure 2: Power-Sharing Models

The voting public ran the military and the civil service in the service of the Kaiser.

Figure B represents a power-sharing relationship in which extensive power-sharing exists between two roughly equal partners. This situation prevailed in the People's Republic of China at the time of the eleventh Party Congress in 1969. The partnership was composed of the People's Liberation Army and the Chinese Communist Party, both of whom were roughly equally represented at the Congress.

Figure C represents a power-sharing relationship in which one of the partners exceeds the other and limited power-sharing exists. It is a situation that reflects the relationship that formerly existed between the Communist Party and the security forces of the USSR. The party dominated the relationship because of its size and responsibilities, which included control of the military and the KGB. The partnership was real, inasmuch as general officers sat on the politburo, playing an active role in strategy making. Moreover, the party could not long exist without the protection of the security forces, whose senior officers enjoyed the privileges of the Communist Party leadership (nomenklatura).

Figure D represents a situation in which the lesser partner exists within the larger member. This relationship exists in the United States, where the body politic greatly exceeds the federal government in strength. The voting public dominates the relationship inasmuch as they determine the national leadership. The military is not included in the power-sharing in a constitutional republic.

Conclusions

Soldiers reflect the political culture of the state. Whereas the soldiers of a constitutional order of a liberal society are law-abiding citizens subject to the civilian authority of the republic; the soldiers of a communist dictatorship are executioners who enforce the authority of an authoritarian police state that exterminates men, women and children designated as enemies of the state (e.g., property owners, clergy, and members of the middle class).

On one hand, soldiers of a constitutional republic demonstrate the freedom loving and law-abiding character of their liberal society. On the other hand, communist soldiers demonstrate the brutal behavior of those called upon to commit crimes against humanity in the name of the state.

Constitutional republics that use soldiers to defend freedom by defending the constitution and the society from external threats have military institutions and forces that mirror the law-abiding conduct of the larger society, as is the case in the USA. Dictatorships such as the People's Republic of China use the People's Liberation Army (PLA) to defend the country as well as to purge enemies of the state within the domestic society. The PLA is a ruthless military force used to carry out crimes against humanity, resulting in a merciless, cruel and callous temperament on the part of the men and women serving in the ranks of the PLA. The differences between the soldiers of the two contrasting political systems are enormous, yet they are never mentioned by progressive apologists for a socialist utopia.

We are what we do is a truism that governs in the formation of character, culture and conduct. Those who kill in the name of the state are killers. Their brutal conduct shapes their character and personal behavior.

Political leaders in the USA allocate resources, make strategy, and are subject to the will of the people who share power through their elected representatives. The American military does not have a role in allocating resources and making strategy, despite widespread belief in the military-industrial complex within the academic community. The charges made by the academic community and liberal media accusing the Pentagon of creating a military-industrial complex as well as strategy making by general officers are false.

General officers share power and have a role in making strategy in authoritarian and totalitarian dictatorships. Consequently, to the extent that the military-industrial complex exists, it is in a military dictatorship, like Spain under Franco's rule, or in a communist dictatorship, like the People's Republic of China—political systems in which the military and internal security forces share power.

Chapter 4:

THE PROXY WAR FOUGHT IN VIETNAM

Legion magazine, the publication of the American Legion, recognized the fiftieth anniversary of the Vietnam War with a series of articles presenting accounts of the war on land, at sea, and in the air. Pieces challenging the historical record highlighted the series. Accounts of the war as taught in our institutions of higher learning were called into question by two striking pieces. "Why We Went to War in Vietnam" by Michael Lind appeared in the January 2013 issue of *Legion*. "The Wrong Side Won" by Uwe Siemon-Netto appeared in the December 2013 issue.

Michael Lind, a distinguished scholar, and senior fellow at the New America Foundation, has written a wide-ranging assessment of the war in *Vietnam: The Necessary War*. Lind's article draws on interviews and published works by leaders from both sides of the conflict—the basis for his landmark study. Lind's *Legion* article avoids moral judgments of the war, seeing it as history to be viewed by scholars with access to records of both sides.

He sees the war as neither a crime nor a mistake, but a proxy war between the United States and the Soviet Union, allied with the People's Republic of China. Lind's account reveals an enormous presence by the Soviet Union and the PRC in the war through wide-ranging support for Hanoi. Lind depicts the war as one conflict of several that called for a resolute response by America to aggressive probing by communist bloc nations.

Lind puts to rest the myth that the war was a civil war. According to Communist Party historian Nguyen Khac Vien, the National Liberation Front was a ruse made up of a group from the Democratic Republic of Vietnam (DRV). The Tet Offensive, seen as an American defeat in the United States, was a devastating defeat for the North, eventually making a conventional victory the only hope for the DRV (i.e., attempts to spark an insurrection of the people against the Saigon regime failed). It was a hope successfully thwarted by the United States and the Government of Vietnam (GVN).

Domestic opposition to the war forced Nixon to seek a settlement based on South Vietnamese self-reliance called Vietnamization and détente with the Soviet Union and the PRC. After the Paris Peace Accords, American forces were withdrawn. Nixon's attempt to achieve peace with honor failed when Congress refused to fund US aid for South Vietnam. The unilateral American capitulation resulted in the conquest of the South by the People's Army of Vietnam (PAVN).

While the United States lost the proxy war, it won the global Cold War. The Soviet Union lost not only the Cold War; it ceased to exist in 1991. Russian historians had concluded that the enormous cost of the proxy war supporting Hanoi was a major cause for the dissolution of the Soviet Union.

Lind notes that there is no evidence that Hanoi ever envisioned a role as a neutral. The North Vietnamese saw themselves as a part of the communist bloc nations and sought support from the Soviet Union and the PRC. By the end of the Cold War, Vietnam had become the Soviet Union's major ally in Asia.

Uwe Siemon-Netto's article in *Legion* takes a more personal look at the war based on his reporting as a German correspondent. He has been based in Saigon and traveled throughout the country. He contests the conventional wisdom that American soldiers are war criminals as maintained by communist bloc nations and the anti-war movement in the West.

Uwe Siemon-Netto found his personal ethic conflicted by reporting of the war. Journalists referred to the invasion of South Vietnam by the North as liberation, although the people never migrated toward North Vietnam or communist-liberated zones.

They fled to areas controlled by the Saigon government. The fear of the communists by the people made clear that what was going on was not liberation. The failure of the press to report this basic truth amounted to journalistic malpractice. Walter Cronkite was one of those he accused of journalistic malpractice. He became convinced that logic became one of the casualties of the war as was intellectual honesty.

He described the terror campaigns waged by the communists murdering those who supported the Republic of Vietnam (RVN). Despite the widespread use of terror by the communists, he found journalists reluctant to report acts of terror unless they were committed by combatants supporting the Saigon government.

Hue, the traditional capital of the country, was the scene of widespread executions during the Tet Offensive. Falsely believing that the Tet Offensive would trigger the overthrow of the Saigon regime, the North threw their entire weight behind the campaign. The communists entered Hue with lists of suspects who were rounded up, tried, and executed. Their crime was supporting the Saigon government, for which they were pronounced guilty by tribunals and executed. Mass graves revealed the bodies of thousands shot in the back of the head.

After the communist defeat, mass graves were uncovered. Uwe covered the story with Peter Braestrup of the *Washington Post*. Both men observed film crews walking aimlessly around but filming nothing. Braestrup asked why they were not filming. They responded, saying, "We are not here to film anticommunist propaganda."

Uwe Siemon-Netto asked why American editors ignored the widespread suffering after the war when millions were sent to gulags, executed, or starved to death. He provided no answers to the question. However, he reported that the vast majority of American and Vietnamese soldiers acted out their vocation in service to others, yet their honorable behavior went unreported. It is a sad commentary that confirms that fake news was alive and well during the Vietnam War.

Siemon-Netto made it clear that communist soldiers carried out mass murders as well as random terrorist attacks to punish popular support for the Saigon regime, which was the policy of North Vietnam. American policy was to protect the population and punish those who violated rules of engagement written for that purpose.

He closes on an optimistic note, saying it may take decades until we see the soldiers' sacrifices in Vietnam bear fruit and the communist regime toppled. Nevertheless, he expresses the hope in the ultimate vindication of the cause of the South Vietnamese people and the Saigon government. His verdict is unmistakable: The wrong side won. The war criminals were the leaders of the North and those who supported their cause.

Chapter 5:

THE PEOPLE'S WAR THE PEOPLE REJECTED

A recently published history reveals events that have transpired in Hanoi during the Vietnam War. Entitled *Hanoi's War: An International History of the War for Peace in Vietnam*, the book chronicles the complex events of the war America waged in Southeast Asia as seen through the eyes of our opponents in North Vietnam. Written by a second-generation Vietnamese American, Lien-Hang T. Nguyen, the book provides detailed accounts of the war based on the official records of the Democratic Republic of Vietnam (DRV) and captured records of the Government of South Vietnam (GVN).[8]

---

[8] Lien-Hang T. Nguyen, Hanoi's War: An International History of the War for Peace in Vietnam (Chapel Hill: The University of North Carolina Press, 2012), 444 pages.

Nguyen has produced an important work based on the official files of the Communist Party, as well as the ministries of the government of the DRV. Her work provides views of stunning clarity on political intrigue, national policies, and Hanoi's war planning never seen before in the West. Among the revelations is the fact that Ho Chi Minh was not the leader of North Vietnam during the war, as many in the West believed at the time.

Ho was the national leader in the war to defeat French colonialism. Le Duan, the Communist Party secretary, was the leader of North Vietnam during the war America waged in support of the GVN. Le Duan was a dedicated man, as ruthless as Stalin or Mao. Far more ruthless than Ho, Le Duan had Ho marginalized in a manner similar to the way Stalin eliminated rivals for power in the USSR.

Ho's sin was to oppose Le Duan's vision for immediate and total victory through a general insurrection to overthrow the GVN. Ho's objection was that Le Duan's immediate liberation of South Vietnam came at the expense of building socialism in North Vietnam. While Ho was removed from office, Le Duan spared his life. Ho's usefulness as a symbol of the revolution saved him from the fate of Leon Trotsky, who was murdered by Stalin while in exile in Mexico.

Another revelation is that the Tet Offensive of 1968 was not a unique countrywide military offensive as seen in the West. It was one of three massive political insurrections intended to overthrow the Saigon government. The insurrections were supported by simultaneous military attacks to destroy the GVN and American military. Known as the general insurrection, the uprising was planned to replicate the popular countrywide insurrection against the French that spontaneously occurred after their return after World War II. The original general insurrection demonstrated massive popular support for the Vietminh and established them as the legitimate national authority.[9]

The problem with the insurrection, or insurrections, planned by Hanoi for South Vietnam was that the people went to ground rejecting the calls of the National Liberation Front (NLF) for an uprising. During the Tet Offensive of 1968, the people sided with the Saigon government, while the communist military attacks were repulsed or destroyed.

Hanoi made three attempts to launch countrywide political insurrections to bring down the Saigon government and expel the Americans. Each of the insurrections was accompanied by multiple military attacks by the Vietcong and the People's Army of Vietnam (PAVN). The three general insurrections were the 1964 general uprising, the 1968 Tet Offensive, and the 1972 Easter Offensive. Occurring at four-year intervals, the insurrections ended in costly failures for Hanoi.

---

[9] The Vietminh was a front organization organized and controlled by the Communist Party (Lao Dong). The Vietminh posed as a coalition of anticolonial political parties that was free and independent. Posing as a united front of parties representing liberal, democratic, and pro-KMT groups, they joined the Vietminh where they were infiltrated and captured by the communists.

In each of the insurrections, the population rejected calls to join with the NLF to take control of villages, district towns, and provincial capitals across the forty-four provinces of South Vietnam. The attacks failed to attract popular support. In each case, the Vietcong and PAVN came out from hiding, exposing their vulnerable ranks to the soldiers, marines, and airmen of the Americans and South Vietnamese military, who shot them down in massive bloodbaths. The few provincial capitals taken by the communists were retaken using American firepower to destroy the outgunned communists.

The failed insurrections were disasters for the NLF and the Communist Party of North Vietnam. The communist leaders believed their own propaganda, expecting the uprising of the entire population as occurred when the French returned after World War II. Instead, the South Vietnamese people rejected the NLF calls for insurrections and went into hiding until the bloodbaths were over. Meanwhile, the Vietcong (VC) and the PAVN sustained devastating losses.

Following orders from the Lao Dong Party (Communist Party of North Vietnam), the VC and PAVN cast off the cover of darkness and the protection of jungle bunkers to face their enemy protected by nothing more than black pajamas or khaki uniforms. They died by the thousands. In many locations, it took American bulldozers to bury the dead in massive graves. Meanwhile, shocked American journalists unaccustomed to combat told their readers back home that America had lost the war—an absurd distortion of the truth.

Nguyen quotes the actual reports contained in the official Communist Party records that document the losses sustained by the NLF, VC, and PAVN in the South. Nguyen's work challenges what we have come to understand as the history of the Vietnam War.

Her work reveals Hanoi was no liberator; rather, it was a conqueror. Hanoi conquered South Vietnam in an exhausting series of offensive campaigns that heavily depleted PAVN ranks, placing enormous demands for replacements on the population of the North. Hanoi's war efforts succeeded at the price of great sacrifices made by the North, as well as by the Soviet Union and the People's Republic of China.

The final offensive to overthrow the Saigon regime was launched in 1975. It was a conventional military campaign consisting of massive PAVN attacks that captured the South after the United States capitulated. The military character of the final offensive revealed that the communists won without a popular insurrection that would have served to legitimize the communist takeover. Hanoi won the war without a popular uprising "to welcome the communist liberators and throw out the capitalists and the puppets of the Americans in Saigon" (Communist propaganda line). The hard truth was that the communist "liberators" were never welcomed by the people of South Vietnam.

Nguyen's book, *Hanoi's War*, reveals a war that differs substantially from accounts of the war published in the West. In view of Hanoi's more accurate account of the situation on the ground in both North and South Vietnam, our appreciation of the war is called into question. Our understanding of the contribution made by the United States and its allies requires substantial revision, given the successive defeats suffered by the North, the VC, and the NLF. Moreover, *Hanoi's War* sheds new light on the character of the Saigon government.

Nguyen's publication of information from Hanoi's classified files and from the captured records of the Saigon regime reveals the tenacity of the leadership of South Vietnam. Contradicting widespread propaganda claiming Saigon was an American puppet, Communist Party appraisals of the GVN showed they were far from puppets. The Republic of Vietnam was a strong sovereign state with its own popular power base, economic base, and battle-tested armed forces, of which they were justly proud. *Hanoi's War* reveals the RVN as a tough opponent capable of mobilizing popular support that presented a difficult challenge to Hanoi's offensives, driving up the costs to unify the country.

The other side of the story was that the North, under the leadership of Le Duan, was a remarkably resilient opponent, dedicated to the power struggle with a formidable tenacity that was clearly illustrated in Nguyen's work. The DRV saw the war through to the end with an expenditure of incalculable human sacrifices and national resources. The sacrifices of the Democratic Republic of Vietnam were accompanied by massive logistical support provided by the USSR and the PRC.

The war was truly a herculean effort. All parties were tested mightily as reflected by the US capitulation and the subsequent collapse of the USSR. Nothing less than the unwavering support of American foreign assistance and the sustained commitment of American air support could have saved the Republic of Vietnam. Regrettably, the American anti-war movement and lack of popular support on the home front ended the American war effort, resulting in an American capitulation and the fall of Saigon.

Hanoi's War is a must read. It provides a balanced and detailed account of the war. Moreover, it gives us an appreciation of the conflict that demonstrates that the Americans and South Vietnamese have jointly achieved far more than they have been given credit for in the West. One day *Hanoi's War* ought to be the basis for the official history of the war in the West.

Chapter 6:

COMMUNISM 101: THE COMMUNIST REVOLUTIONARY MODELS

On the friendly side of the front lines, "community organizer" is a new job description that Americans were unfamiliar with during the wars to contain communism— the Cold War, the Korean War, and the Vietnam War. On the enemy side of the lines, the term has long been a well-respected job title.

"Community organizer" was the name given to the front men and women who were the vanguard of the communist revolutionary movement. The community organizers were communist cadre who penetrated capitalist societies to organize the workers' revolt. It was dangerous work in countries like South Vietnam, where the people were alert to the threat of communist revolt and revolution.

The two great community organizers who pioneered communist revolutionary warfare were Vladimir Ilyich Lenin and Mao Zedong. Lenin led the Russian October Revolution of 1917 as the leader of the Bolshevik Party. Mao led the peasants' revolution in China that captured control of Peking in 1949, establishing the model for communist revolution in agrarian societies.

The Russian Revolution

Our story of Lenin begins in Switzerland. It was during the First World War when travel in central Europe was difficult and dangerous. Lenin was participating in the Second International (International Workingmen's Association) as the senior Bolshevik representative to the Conference. Lenin and the Bolsheviks were in exile at the time. (The Bolshevik deputies to the Russian Duma had been exiled from Russia for opposing tax credits for Russian participation in the First World War.)

It was in Switzerland that Lenin learned of the abdication of the Tsar and the formation of the Kerensky government. Known as the March Revolution of 1917, it signaled the end of the Romanov Dynasty. Lenin knew his leadership was needed in Saint Petersburg. The Bolsheviks were committed to carrying out an uprising that required Lenin's presence to direct a workers' revolution. It would be a revolution that would bring the Bolsheviks to power in a communist coup.

Lenin went to the German embassy where he asked for assistance in traveling across Germany to return to Russia. The Germans had been following Lenin's movement. They recognized Lenin posed a serious threat to Russian political stability.

Recognizing an opportunity to undermine the new Russian government, the Germans offered Lenin safe passage for himself and his Bolshevik comrades as well as financial support. Lenin accepted the offer that made him a German agent. German support for the Russian revolutionaries became public knowledge. It would alienate Russian allies but was instrumental in taking Russia out of the First World War. [10]

Lenin took control of the Bolshevik Party in Saint Petersburg and led the October Revolution of 1917. Under the slogan of all power to the Soviets, the move was perceived as a grass roots revolt that went unopposed by the other political parties in the Duma. In alliance with the Garrison of Saint Petersburg and sailors of the Baltic Fleet, the Bolsheviks seized control of the Russian capitol on the night of 7 November 1917, overthrowing the Kerensky government.

Following the capture of Saint Petersburg, the Bolsheviks formed an army of peasants and workers that was known as the Red Army. Under Leon Trotsky's leadership, the Red Army fought a long and brutal civil war to capture control of the Russian state. We recognize the Bolshevik revolution

---

[10] Richard Pipes, *Communism: A History* (New york,2001), pg. 37.

as the Leninist model of revolution that became the prototype for subsequent workers' revolutions.

Lenin formed the Third International. Known as the "Comintern," it served as the communist control center for directing the world-wide revolution of the working class. After Lenin's death, Josef Stalin, the Party Secretary of the Soviet Union, became the head of the Comintern.

Contrary to Soviet Red Army experience using peasant soldiers and factory workers to wage war, Stalin directed a return to the teachings of Karl Marx and reliance upon factory workers to carry out the class struggle. It was an unfortunate move for many community organizers in the Third World, where factory workers were not a part of the work force.

The Chinese Communist Revolution

Following the collapse of the Manchu Dynasty in 1911, the Chinese Nationalists or Kuomintang (KMT) ruled China under the leadership of Sun Yat-sen. An admirer of Lenin's rise to power in the Soviet Union, Sun Yat-sen received communist advisors from the Comintern to assist the KMT. The Comintern concurrently encouraged the formation of the Chinese Communist Party (CCP) that was formed in 1921. After a period of collaboration, the KMT, and CCP became bitter rivals. The two rivals fought four wars from 1924 until 1949 to defeat local war lords, oppose foreign invasion, and win the right to claim power as the legitimate ruler of China.

The First Revolutionary Civil War (1924-1927) saw the CCP allied with the KMT against regional war lords to unify China. The Second Revolutionary Civil War (1927 -1937) saw the KMT fighting Mao's peasant army in the Kiangsi base area. The United Front Period (1937 to 1945) saw the CCP, and the KMT united against the invasion of the Imperial Japanese Army. The Third Revolutionary Civil War (1945-1949) saw the CCP consolidate control over China, defeat the KMT, and capture the seat of government at Peking.

During their joint campaign to unify China, the CCP, and the KMT enjoyed considerable success organizing peasants to resist regional war lords. Given effective leadership, the common people were ready to revolt. The peasants had endured famine, a shattered economy, abuses by colonial powers, and oppression by local war lords. Mao recognized the great potential for mobilizing the communist revolution based entirely on the support of the large peasant population of rural China. Mao concentrated all his recruiting efforts on the formation of peasant military units.

The CCP was following the directives of the Comintern. They directed Mao to concentrate on recruiting workers. Ignoring the CCP leadership, Mao targeted all his recruiting efforts on mobilizing peasants. It made no sense to try to recruit factory workers in an impoverished agrarian society. The Comintern Party line was incorrect for agrarian societies like China with extraordinarily little industry. The policy resulted in costly failures at the hands of the Nationalists under Chiang Kai-shek, who had succeeded Sun Yat-sen as leader of the KMT.

During the Second Revolutionary Civil War, the Nationalists conducted five bandit extermination campaigns to destroy Mao's peasant armies. Chiang was assisted by German military advisors, who helped the Nationalists inflict heavy losses upon Mao's peasant forces. Mao was forced to abandon the Kiangsi base area and flee to escape total annihilation. The Red Army carried out the Long March, a long difficult trek that necessitated repeated rear-guard battles. Numbering 90,000 peasant soldiers upon their departure, Mao's force was reduced to 20,000 men by the time they reached their destination at Shensi in remote northern China.

After a bitter internal struggle within the CCP and ten long years of civil war with the KMT, the fortunes of the CCP reached their lowest point. Party leaders fought over the character of the communist revolution. When the Party was founded in 1921, the CCP was committed to the Leninist model of revolution. Sixteen years later, much had changed. The revolution was peasant based, and efforts to organize factory workers had been abandoned. The CCP and the Red Army had become one. Mao had been recognized as the sole leader and appointed Chairman of the Chinese Communist Party.

During their long struggle, the communist movement had evolved into a disciplined peasant army that had taken the name of the People's Liberation Army (PLA). The Party cadre under Mao's leadership had become expert community organizers. The Party cadre used land reform and patriotism to rally support among the peasants. It was a time of dramatic change. The murdering of landowners occasioned by land reform gave the peasant mobilization a militant character that Mao called, creating political power from the barrel of a gun.

While the CCP battled to mobilize the peasantry, much had changed in the international community. The Japanese had invaded China. The KMT was pushed out of northern China and the coastal cities. The Soviet Union was threatened by Nazi Germany. And the Anti-Comintern Pact threatened the international communist movements as well as the western democracies. The Comintern called for a United Front with the democracies to meet the threat posed by Fascism.

Mao proposed a United Front with the KMT to oppose the Japanese invasion. Chiang Kai-shek refused an alliance with the CCP but was forced to accept a United Front when confronted by the savagery of the Japanese invasion, as well as the appeals for unity by northern war lords and the Communists. The United Front made the CCP eligible for American military assistance. Mao was joined by American military advisors at his command center at Yan'an in northern China.

Based upon their findings, the American advisors provided the US War Department with a blueprint of Mao's organization from top to bottom. They recorded the tactics and strategy employed by the PLA. Their findings were recorded in the U.S. War Department Report of the Military Intelligence Division dated 5 July 1945. Congressional recognition of the importance of the report resulted in the incorporation of the report in the Congressional record. [11]

Mao's community organizers built a rival clandestine government that replaced the official government of the KMT. The CCP community organizers built the communist organization from the village level to the district, province, and national levels. At each echelon, the revolutionary structures included militia units, a government counsel (National Defense Association), Communist Party cell(s), and units of the People's Liberation Army. The community organizations contained all the elements of the communist revolutionary movement.

Whereas the Japanese invasion was a disaster for the KMT, it was a windfall victory for the CCP. The invasion of the Japanese Imperial Army drove the Nationalists out of northern China, central China, and the coastal cities. The Japanese did not have the manpower to garrison the vast areas abandoned by the KMT. The Japanese occupied the coastal cities, but they left the hinterlands unoccupied. The PLA fought to take possession of the abandoned territory, to secure base areas, and to eliminate any remaining vestiges of the Japanese and the KMT.

---

[11] Andrew P. O'Meara, Jr., *Infrastructure and the Marxist Power Seizure* (New York: Vantage Press, 1973) pages 45-46.

The Third Revolutionary Civil War (1945 to 1949) was an uneven contest. By the end of the United Front, the CCP governed much of rural China. Their armies greatly outnumbered the forces of the KMT. With U.S. support Nationalist military forces occupied the cities surrendered by the Japanese, but they were soon surrounded and cut off by the PLA that controlled the countryside. The PLA starved out the cities garrisoned by the KMT, taking the surrender of millions of KMT soldiers. The Americans offered to negotiate the formation of a coalition government of China, which had no chance of success and was declined. Peking was captured in 1949 in an empty, but diplomatically symbolic gesture of victory by the CCP.

Unlike Lenin's October revolution, the CCP had no need for a coup to capture the national government. They had independently built the Chinese government one village and one province at a time. The capture of Peking in 1949 was strictly a symbolic gesture to announce to the world that the CCP was in charge of China. (The CCP continues to use the political structure built during the revolution.)

Mao's model of revolution was not a workers' revolution. It was built with the support of the peasants of an agrarian society. Unlike the Soviet experience, the civil war occurred before the capture of the national government. The CCP established control of most of rural China by the end of the United Front Period. Mao's peasants' revolution became the model for communist revolutions in agrarian societies.

Revolutionary Models

Lenin and Mao were the founders of the two different revolutionary models for waging communist revolutionary warfare. Lenin was credited with organizing the first workers' revolution, putting into practice the doctrine of Karl Marx. It became the primary model of Marxist revolution in industrial societies that consisted of a coup to seize the government, followed by a civil war to capture the state. The Russian Revolution was expected to be the first of many workers' revolts to carry out a world-wide workers' revolution to destroy capitalism.

Mao's community-organizing efforts in China created a new approach to carry out a communist revolution that was based on a grassroots approach to gain control of the people and the state, followed by the eventual fall of the government. Mao's efforts built an underground communist government that was already controlling most of China when they captured Peking in 1949.

Mao's approach was carried out by organizing the People's Liberation Army, local militia, the Communist Party, and governing bodies in liberated areas. Mao's decentralized approach took control of China one village and one province at a time until the entire rural countryside was communist controlled. Unlike the Russian Revolution, the Chinese Civil War and seizure of control of the state occurred in China before the seizure of the central government of the Chinese nationalists in 1949.

The Vietminh

Opportunities to export Mao's model of revolution followed hard on the heels of World War II. Organizing communist parties had already begun by the Comintern in Southeast Asia by the formation of communist party organizations in Vietnam, Cochin China, Annam, Cambodia, and Laos. These party organizations became the foundations for building the revolution on the efforts of community organizers.

The Lao Dong Party, the Communist Party of Vietnam, launched its war to drive out the French colonial administration upon the return of the French after the war. To unify the many political parties in Vietnam in a common war effort against the French, the Vietnamese Communist Party formed a united front. They called their united front the Vietminh, which became the voice of the entire people of Vietnam. It was a front controlled by the Communist Party that took control of the revolution, ruthlessly murdering the leadership of other groups that joined the united front.

Chinese military advisers from the People's Liberation Army were dispatched by Mao to aid the Vietminh. They brought with them their experiences fighting the KMT and the Japanese Imperial Army. The PLA taught the Vietnamese to use tunnel warfare employed against the Japanese. And most importantly, they furnished the Vietminh with their blueprint for contesting the countryside by taking political control of the population one village at a time.

The key to the PLA blueprint for control of the villages were the community organizers, who were the first to enter a village. Their business was to organize the four structures of the communist revolution: Party cells, the local militia, the Red Army, and liberation associations that became the nucleus of the rural government. Community organizers were often accompanied by militia who made short work of political opponents of the communists.

The Vietminh revolution culminated in the Battle of Dien Bien Phu, in which a large French military fortress was forced to surrender. The fortified complex was positioned to block infiltration of military aid from communist China. It was far from French support in Hanoi. It was an audacious plan that misjudged the capabilities of the Vietminh reinforced by PLA support. The PLA provided the Vietminh with American artillery to bombard the French into surrender, forcing the French to evacuate North Vietnam.

The National Liberation Front

South Vietnam remained under French control after the French withdrawal from North Vietnam in 1954. It had a civilian government headed by Pres. Ngo Dinh Diem. America offered support to the government of South Vietnam, which became a bastion of anticommunism that was reinforced by over a million refugees from North Vietnam fleeing the Vietminh.

The American support was predicated on the French withdrawal from their former colony. The French left behind a small military contingent composed of a South Vietnamese army, air force, and navy that were trained by the French. American support for South Vietnam included economic aid and military support in the form of advisers and military hardware needed to build up the armed forces.

North Vietnam launched a war to unify themselves with South Vietnam in 1959. It was concealed behind the National Liberation Front, founded by a group of North Vietnamese communist cadre. The NLF gave the appearance of an independent political front waging a civil war against the Saigon government. They were augmented by the Vietcong, a peasant militia formed to take the war to the South Vietnamese military and their anti-communist government.

Behind the scenes, the Communist Party directed the war from North Vietnam using the blueprint used by the Vietminh in North Vietnam and by the CCP in China. Community organizers, once again, were the vanguard leading the revolution by forming peasant resistance in the villages of South Vietnam. The blueprint that worked for the Vietminh encountered resistance in South Vietnam.

The Vietminh had revealed their hand during the war to drive out the French. They were exposed as murderers who had come to kill property owners, merchants, and those who supported the government. Consequently, the war in the South failed to achieve the results of the Vietminh or the CCP. The South Vietnamese people resisted the communist "liberation." In the end, the North Vietnamese overthrew the government of South Vietnam with an invasion of conventional military forces conducting massive attacks using artillery and tanks to destroy the resistance of South Vietnam. By 1975, the communists were successful, but their method had changed. The model that had worked when largely unopposed in China failed in South Vietnam.

Attack of the VCI

The U.S. CIA directed the attack of the communist community organizers in South Vietnam. Known as the Phoenix Program, the CIA program was extraordinarily successful eliminating the VC community organizers from the countryside by 1972. The military response directed by the CIA was coupled with land reform. The American economic development program bought up large estates that were broken up, and the land was distributed to peasant farmers. The large increase in the number of small landowners created substantial grassroots opposition to NLF recruiting and attempts to abolish private property.

Unfortunately, U.S. attacks of communist cadre had a rough start as the Americans learned through costly trial and error to wage the clandestine war. During the Kennedy administration, employment of U.S. Army Special Forces (SF) was recognized as the logical response to carry out attacks on the VCI. Accordingly, Army Special Forces were expanded and directed to take out the communist cadre. Their efforts met with stiff resistance from Army lawyers, who saw their actions as murder.

The lawyers had no tolerance for tit-for-tat assassinations of enemy terrorists carried out by the Americans in response to the purge of class enemies by communist community organizers. [12] The selective targeting of community cadre for elimination by the SF met the definition of murder according to the Uniform Code of Military Justice (UCMJ) according to the Army AG community. After several cases in which successful VCI attacks resulted in the prosecution of SF leaders for murder, it was clear that American soldiers were not the solution to combat the communist cadre. Reluctantly, the Army assigned new missions to Special Forces units. After a costly false start, American leaders were forced to seek other solutions to cope with NLF community organizers.

SF units were directed to assist mountain tribesmen resisting the communist presence in the South Vietnamese highlands. The SF also conducted surveillance of enemy supply operations along the Ho Chi Minh Trail. The new missions were consistent with the original purpose of the Special Forces. The infiltration of PAVN men and supplies

---

[12]The American cultural bias against anything resembling the employment of unlawful use of force in Vietnam was clearly demonstrated. The unfounded charges by the VVAW of widespread atrocities committed by Americans were entirely false.

into the South became far more expensive for Hanoi once the SF took over the new missions. Although the SF were effective in their new roles, valuable time had been lost responding to the threat posed by communist community organizers.

The solution to attacks by VC community organizers on the civilian population was to allow the Vietnamese people to defend their own villages. Local militia units were formed to create armed resistance at the village level. Known as regional and provincial forces (RF/PF), the program armed the rural population to defend their villages. Provincial Reconnaissance Units (PRU) composed of former Viet Cong solders were organized to take the attack against enemy cadre in communist controlled villages. Dressed in black pajamas, the PRU could pass for VC militia, allowing them to penetrate communist liberated areas with impunity. By 1972, the RF/ PF militia and the Phoenix Program had cleaned the vast majority of the countryside of NLF community organizers.

The CIA had played a major role in the attack of the VCI. The CIA developed the Phoenix Program to orchestrate the multi-agency program employing exclusively Vietnamese assets. Vietnamese Special Forces, GVN national police, and GVN district level administrations collaborated to carry out the work. The RF/ PF militia that armed the local populace ensured that when *political power came from the barrel of a gun in accordance with Mao's doctrine*, the gun was in friendly hands. The GVN district headquarters functioned as the central focus of local VCI intelligence collection. The attack was in the hands of the GVN, including apprehension and interrogation of suspects, incarceration of prisoners, and assassination attempts. Once the Program was instituted, the local success experienced served as a catalyst to ensure the final victory over the communist cadre.

With the defeat of the NLF at the village level, Hanoi was faced with the prospect of complete failure. The defeat of the revolutionary cadre coupled with the defeat of the Easter Offensive of 1972 threatened to terminate Hanoi's war to unify the country in failure. The PAVN had experienced catastrophic losses from determined ARVN resistance and B-52 strikes during the Easter Offensive. The decisive combat occurred in the highlands where a major effort was made to take An Loc.

A provincial capitol located on the Cambodian border, An Loc was an important symbol of GVN authority. The loss of An Loc by Saigon would have handed Hanoi a major victory to crown what had been a dismal failure to over-throw the Saigon Government by a general insurrection. The problem was the ARVN defense of An Loc withstood a lengthy siege and the PAVN units were forced to retreat to escape punishing B-52 strikes.

Following their defeat at An Loc, what remained of the PAVN forces withdrew to sanctuaries in Cambodia and in the central highlands to rest, refit and take stock of their predicament. They were in the thirteenth year of a war to liberate South Vietnam. It had been a long, expensive, and very bloody war that appeared to have ended in defeat. Hanoi had little to show for their herculean efforts, and there was little incentive to continue a war that had demanded enormous sacrifices from the Vietnamese people.

PAVN had been devastated. Replacements were needed to fill the ranks of the exhausted infantry units. Additionally, massive foreign assistance was needed to replace the weapons and equipment destroyed in combat. To make matters worse, the revolutionary cadre of the NLF had suffered country wide defeats. It appeared the time had come to accept the judgment of the people of the South, who had rejected all attempts at "liberation" by Hanoi.

While the situation was dismal from the perspective of those defeated in the South, the international situation was encouraging. Second fronts against the war in America and Europe offered strong support for the DRV. The American anti-war movement had reached a fever pitch, while similar efforts in Europe attracted wide support and were the subject of intense media coverage.

American opposition to the war resulted in the election of an anti-war Congress that passed legislation making it unlawful to provide logistical or air support for our allies in South Vietnam. It amounted to a total capitulation by the Americans. Given the collapse of American support for the Saigon regime, Hanoi made the decision to continue the war for the defeat of the Saigon regime of South Vietnam.

A reversal of fortunes like those Mao experienced following the Japanese invasion of China had come to the rescue of Hanoi. With massive support from Communist China and the Soviet Union, Hanoi rebuilt the PAVN forces crippled in the Easter Offensive. In addition to training large contingents of new recruits to fill the ranks of shattered infantry divisions, Hanoi reorganized homeland defense forces to build up combat units available to support the final offensive.

The end of American bombing of the DRV permitted a massive redeployment of homeland defense forces. PAVN divisions released from duty defending the North were reassigned to strengthen the final offensive. Engineer and infantry units protecting the rail links to China and the Ho Chi Minh Trail were redeployed to augment the final offensive.

Air defense artillery units no longer required for the protection of Hanoi and Haiphong were converted to field artillery and redeployed to expand combat reserves for the final offensive.

The final offensive was launched with massive attacks of PAVN units equipped with modern Soviet tanks and artillery. Their offensive simultaneously struck ARVN units deployed along the Seventeenth Parallel, in the Central Highlands, and in the ARVN Third Corps sector defending Saigon.

ARVN troop units fought bravely, but with little hope of success given the limited stocks of munitions remaining in the country. The collapse of resistance in the First Corps sector signaled the beginning of the end. Hanoi's efforts were crowned with success when Saigon was captured on 30 April 1975. It had been an offensive of conventional forces without the support of the civilian population. Despite Hanoi's final victory, People's war had suffered a humiliating setback. With the failure of the general insurrection (Easter Offensive), it was clear that community organizers had failed in South Vietnam.

The Revolution in the USA

The Communist Party USA (CPUSA) has a long history of waging the power struggle in America. It has penetrated top echelons of the government. Its activities include facilitating espionage, planting disinformation, disseminating propaganda, and organizing political action groups designed to wage the political struggle. Community organizers are an important part of their work.

The CPUSA suffers from the misfortune of attempting to launch a Marxist revolution in a society that enjoys one of the highest standards of living in the world, which serves as a damper on revolutionary zeal (i.e., they have a hard time recruiting true workers). It is an irony that has tended to skew recruiting away from labor and into student groups that tend to be more susceptible to communist indoctrination.

Given the diversity of opinions, authorities, and revolutionary models, we see evidence of multiple approaches simultaneously competing for relevance in our fractured civic culture. In addition to efforts to apply the Leninist and Maoist models of revolution in America, we find an original political theory adapted to a complex American political culture.

Saul Alinsky has written *Rules for Radicals*, which attempts to reconfigure the Marxist doctrine to the environment found in America. Alinsky who called himself a community organizer directed Marxist revolutionaries to conceal their intentions and penetrate the political system to destroy the values, institutions, and structures that sustain the society. Alinsky advocated penetrating the federal and state governments to accumulate the power to destroy the republic, which the Left calls boring from within.

Although Alinsky has passed away, his work goes on without him.

In addition to community organizers like Saul Alinsky, the CPUSA has been assisted in mobilizing support for radical social change by progressive educators, who have popularized socialist teachings of European philosophers. The socialist claims of social justice through redistribution of wealth have had great appeal for idealistic professors and naïve students, despite the tragic consequences experienced by Marxist revolutions based on the Leninist and Maoist models of revolution.

One of the most influential educators advocating socialist reforms was John Dewey. While not a community organizer, Dewey greatly facilitated their work by spreading socialist beliefs. Dewey taught at Columbia

University. During the1930's Dewey was instrumental in placing expatriate German educators in teaching positions at American universities. The German educators had fled Nazi persecution that had become a serious threat to the Jewish community.

The German expatriates were from the Frankfurt School, a prominent left-wing university and proponent of critical theory. A Marxist concept, critical theory, taught sophisticated methods to over-throw liberal governments of societies where the workers rejected the revolution. Critical theory taught that liberal societies with free market economies must be broken by deconstruction of their national heritage and institutions. Vilification of the national heritage made the people more susceptible to the appeals of communism. The teaching of critical theory from the Frankfurt School produced revisionist history and identity politics that have greatly influenced Left-wing politics in America.

The German expatriates taught at Columbia, Harvard, Brandeis, and University of California, San Diego. They targeted discontented individuals on the fringes of society, who were considered ripe for recruitment by the radical Left. They appealed to the Bohemian community, as well as sexually repressed individuals and persecuted minorities.

Herbert Marcuse, the most famous German expatriate, taught what has been called identity socialism. Marcuse introduced tolerance of intolerance, which inverted social norms (i.e., persecuted minorities and the sexually repressed were to be tolerated, but privileged members of society were not to be tolerated). His ideas were instrumental in advancement of identity politics that have become the center of radical politics in America.

Two militant groups, Antifa, and Black Lives Matter (BLM), have emerged as the vanguard of the ongoing revolutionary struggle. Both organizations seek to destroy the civic structures of the existing government as called for by critical theory. They have staged large protest demonstrations that have turned into violent riots in major cities across the U.S.

Antifa is a radical Marxist group that employs fascist-like violence to destroy rivals and political opponents. Antifa has been designated a terrorist organization by the Department of Justice, while BLM is not far behind. BLM has carried out campaigns to bring down municipal authorities by attacking the police. Both Antifa and BLM oppose funding for the police. Both adhere to strictly Marxist agendas.

Antifa has its origin in Europe following World War I. It was first identified in Italy associated with resistance to the Italian fascist movement controlled by Benito Mussolini. It later appeared in Germany in opposition to Adolph Hitler and the German National Socialist movement (Nazi). The European Antifa opposition groups were Moscow directed Marxists that opposed rival socialist and fascist political parties.

Speaking at 2020 Independence Day celebrations, President Donald J. Trump described the radical left in

America as fascist activity of a totalitarian movement working to over-throw the constitutional republic formed by the founders in 1776. His remarks make it clear that the CPUSA and its affiliates have achieved recognition as a serious revolutionary movement that is waging a civil war in America as predicted by Gertrude Himmelfarb in her seminal work on political philosophy, *The Roads to Modernity: The British, the French, and the American Enlightenments.*

Who Are Community Organizers?

A century after the October Revolution, when Bolsheviks seized control of Saint Petersburg and overthrew the Kerensky Government, Communism has spread across the world.

Whereas Karl Marx predicted a world-wide workers' revolution beginning in Germany, the revolution of the proletariat has morphed into a peasants' revolution in undeveloped third world countries. Contrary to Marxist doctrine, Communism has not created a workers' paradise. On the contrary, it has resulted in mass murder and totalitarian dictatorships.

The failure of radical community organizers to produce a true workers' revolution, the foundation of Marxist theory, demonstrates the fallacy of Marxist doctrine. The class struggle, the workers' revolution and the downfall of capitalism are not preordained by history as predicted by

Karl Marx. While Marx claimed his theory of world revolution was scientific and based on inevitable forces of history, it is now clear that Karl Marx was wrong and Marxist theory is false.

History plays no favorites. There is no arc of history that makes the transition from capitalism to communism inevitable. Paradise on earth was a pipe dream of Karl Marx, an exiled German expatriate pursuing sanctuary in England, who was entirely out of touch with reality. The only clear result of implementation of Marxist doctrine has been the transformation of terrorists into tyrants, the mass murder of entire social classes, and the subjugation of the working class as slaves of the communist party.

Based upon the record of communist instigated revolutions over the last century we recognize community organizers as the vanguard of the communist party. They do not come as allies of the people of the United States. They come as enemies of the people who have dedicated their lives to the destruction of the free enterprise system and the American constitutional Republic. They constitute a clear and present danger to the Constitution and the life, liberty, and the pursuit of happiness of the American people.

Chapter 7:

PLAYING THE RACE CARD

Several years ago, Martin O'Malley confronted black demonstrators, nearly causing a race riot.[13] The activists were chanting, "Black lives matter." O'Malley said, "All lives matter. White lives matter. Black lies matter." The remarks sounded harmless. Yet black activists objected, and O'Malley was forced to retract them, saying, "Black lives matter." His correction implied that white lives don't really matter. The brouhaha over Martin O'Malley's remarks is enlightening.

The chant of the black demonstrators implies that white lives don't matter, an assertion that denies the fundamental right enunciated in the Declaration of Independence that all men are created equal.[14] The chant of the black demonstrators is a challenge to Conservatives

---

[13] Martin O'Malley was an attorney and the sixty-first governor of Maryland.

[14] The statement is intended to say that all men and women are equal.

denying the fundamental right to equality of white American citizens. How have Americans arrived at this conclusion that denies a fundamental right contained in the founding document of the republic? The truth is, we no longer agree on a common social contract in America. Two alien cultures exist simultaneously in American society, a house divided to use Lincoln's words, an unstable condition that cannot long endure.

The Social Contract Denied

The traditional American social contract is captured in the Pledge of Allegiance school children recite: *I pledge allegiance to the flag of the United States of America and to the republic for which it stands, one nation under God, indivisible with liberty and justice for all*. Unfortunately, the Pledge of Allegiance is no longer honored by all Americans. Some athletes kneel rather than stand when the national anthem is played at sporting events as a public display of rejection of the American flag and the republic for which it stands. We have become two separate people practicing different faiths and loyal to different doctrines.

We have become two peoples or nations in one state, separated by alien cultures that are mutually exclusive. The conflicting cultures have resulted in a divided house. It took a great Civil War to reconstitute *one nation* in Lincoln's day. That *one nation* is the republic formed by the founding fathers and created by the Declaration of Independence and the Constitution of the United States of America.

The other nation—let's call it the *Progressive nation*—has been founded by Progressive reformers who have carved out a new nation within the Democratic Party, the academic community, and the K-12 educational system. It has its own ethos and its own system of morality spelled out in politically correct rules, binding people with threats of shame and excommunication. The PC rules are enforced by Democrats, educators, the liberal media, and Hollywood.

Theirs is a doctrine spelled out by socialist teachings religiously observed by the academic community. It is a doctrine that denigrates American heritage and impugns the traditional American way of life. The challenge America faces is the socialist doctrine poses a threat to the republic. Socialism and the Constitution are mutually exclusive. The problem is compounded by the fact that the Progressive reforms contain fundamental errors—errors that threaten America with rebellion now and ultimately economic ruin.

Socialist Doctrine

The *Progressive nation* was founded by Progressive reformers who adopted socialist views that were incorporated into the educational system beginning in the late nineteenth-century. The reforms were based on the socialist doctrine of Karl Marx and the anticolonial teachings of V. I. Lenin.

They assert that American heritage is fatally flawed. Their revisionist histories accuse our fathers of criminal behavior. They accuse America of being an outlaw nation. They make their case against our republic in the textbooks used in our schools and colleges. The Progressive reformers have subverted our educational system by teaching a revolutionary doctrine, converting education into a weapon against our republic.

Within the Progressive academic community, our children learn that capitalists in the industrialized countries of the West steal the wages of workers as taught by Karl Marx. They learn that the wealth of colonial countries was stolen by the West in accordance with the teachings of V. I. Lenin. The USA is condemned as a criminal capitalist society, which is compounded by Lenin's claim that the USA is a criminal neocolonial country. It is a doctrine that places a twofold curse on Western industrialized societies, such as the USA.

The Black Lives Matter movement adheres to these socialist beliefs. They believe that Americans steal wages from black workers and the wealth of people of color in impoverished third world countries to enrich the West. They hold these doctrines to be true because that is what they have been taught in American schools and Progressive colleges and universities.

The Black Lives Matter Movement

Black Lives Matter (BLM) was formed by three black activists following the acquittal of George Zimmerman for the murder of Trayvon Martin in July 2013. The women (Patrisse Khan-Cullors, Opal Tometi, and Alicia Garza) admit to being trained Marxists dedicated to the abolition of capitalism. A primary goal of BLM is to eliminate racism reflected by the large number of blacks imprisoned in federal and state prisons. BLM's Philadelphia leader has demanded all police departments and prisons must be gone in five years.[15]

BLM advocates the use of active measures (violence) to combat what they see as police brutality. Their chants (e.g., *Pigs in a blanket, Fry 'em like bacon*) have earned them the reputation of being a terrorist group advocating the assassination of police officers. Speaking on Fox News, Hawk Newsome of BLM declared that "If this country doesn't give us what we want then we will burn down the system and replace it." [16]

Police responses to deadly force resulting in the deaths of black offenders have sparked riots that have increased the visibility of BLM. The vilification of police officers involved by Pres. Obama and the refusal of local officials to enforce

---

[15] Rowan Scarborough, "BLM Ideology merges with Marx, Mao rule," *The Washington Times* (August 3, 2020).
[16] *op. cit.*

the law have resulted in riots, looting, and the murder of police officers. Extensive media coverage of the mayhem has resulted in spreading the reputation of BLM and a surge in recruitment across the country.

The case against systemic racism is presented by independent studies. Heather MacDonald, the Thomas W. Smith Fellow at the Manhattan Institute, is author of the NYT Best Seller, *The War Against Cops* (Encounter Books: 2016). In her best-selling book, MacDonald presents FBI crime statistics that show the charge of racism based upon the number of blacks imprisoned in America is untrue.

The data clearly demonstrates the problem of large black prison populations is the result of the high black crime rate, specifically the number of crimes committed by black criminals against the black community. In addition, MacDonald documents the Ferguson Effect whereby police departments under attack reduce their presence in the communities that contest their presence.

MacDonald records the provocation of racial hatred and incitement of violence against law enforcement officers by members of BLM. Given their bloodthirsty activities, the name of the group is misleading. The group benefits significantly from their honorable title. It is a deception of BLM's founders who intentionally hid evil intentions behind a righteous name. "Black Lives Matter" is an unimpeachable truth supported by one and all; whereas BLM's terrorist activities are an evil supported by only the most criminal extremists of the hard Left. The use of an honorable name for terrorists provides semantic cover for deadly attacks upon law enforcement officers.

The everyday use of BLM's misleading title furthers the deception. To level the playing field, GOP officials at the state and local levels should adopt a descriptive name to accurately reflect the character of the Marxist rebels. A name such as Communist Cop Killers (CCK) would deny semantic cover to dangerous criminals. Law enforcement agencies should make a practice of using only the official name (CCK), ignoring hysterical objections from the Left. Over time, the association of the terrorists with their heinous deeds will diminish the group's popularity with law-abiding citizens.

Prisons have large populations of black prisoners because blacks commit far more crimes than any other group in the country. The data is so skewed that BLM and the liberal media will not discuss the subject. Those who mention the official FBI crime rate data are accused of racism to silence the discussion.

Meanwhile, the political pressure brought to bear on the law enforcement community and widespread assassination attempts against police officers have reduced the police presence in local communities. As a result, the war against cops has served to curtail police presence in black neighborhoods, which in turn has led to increased crime in the black community. The irony of the BLM intervention is that it has served to increase crimes committed against those it claims to uphold and protect.

Marx's Theory of Class Warfare

Karl Marx was born on 5 May 1818 in Trier that was part of Prussia at the time. Marx's father, Heinrich Marx was a lawyer. Prussian anti-Semitic bias forced Heinrich Marx to change the family religion to enhance his opportunities for promotion. A Prussian Royal decree of 1816 had denied Jew's promotions to senior positions in the legal and medical professions.[17]

Karl Marx aspired to be a university professor. He studied philosophy at the University of Berlin. Anti-Semitism that was on the rise in Prussia resulted in his rejection for award of a graduation diploma, which precluded a teaching post at the university[18]. Marx was forced to accept a diploma from the University of Jena, a smaller and less prestigious university. The teaching position at the university that Marx coveted was offered to less gifted German undergraduates.

Karl Marx fled the German Rhineland during the Revolutions of 1848, moving to France and later to England, where he settled in London. Marx was provided sanctuary by the London Museum, where he wrote about social problems created by the Industrial Revolution.

---

[17] Paul Johnson, *Intellectuals*, (Harper's Perennials, London, 1988) page 53.

[18] Before the unification of Germany, Berlin was the capitol of Prussia, the most important military power of the German states.

Marx recognized German labor as the vulnerable center of the industrialized German states. His work targeted the solidarity of the labor force. Marx made the case that workers were victims of injustices that arose from class conflicts. Workers were victims of the greed of the owners of industry who stole their wages. *Das Kapital* presented Marx's theory of exploitation of the working class that justified revolution and elimination of class enemies—the wealthy owners of industry (capitalists).

A workers' revolt posed a serious threat to the stability of the German states. It was a problem Germans recognized and addressed with liberal wages, medical care, and retirement benefits. Marx's theory, published as *Das Kapital*, advocated revolution and purging of capitalists. It was his revenge against powerful German nationalists who had denied him the social standing that accompanied a position at the university.

His theory was well received and was adopted by social reformers who championed Marx's call for a worldwide workers' revolution that was expected to start in Germany. Inconveniently, Marx missed his target by hundreds of miles. Instead of igniting a German workers' revolution, the Marxist doctrine triggered the Russian October Revolution of 1917. It was a revolution of Russian workers and peasants led by the Bolshevik Party that overthrew the Kerensky government. A revolutionary government was formed—the Union of Soviet Socialist Republics.

The traditional Russian society and the Kerensky government were destroyed. The power seizure of the Russian government in Saint Petersburg was followed by a long civil war to destroy class enemies and capture control of the Russian state.

The Bolsheviks killed property owners, the nobility, the clergy, and the middle class, effectively eliminating the best educated and industrious members of Russian society. Industry and agriculture were reorganized as a state-controlled economy. Industry was placed under the control of communist managers. Agriculture was collectivized into communes, in which the people worked for state commissars.

It is estimated that, in the process of purging class enemies, seven million peasants were murdered as kulaks—peasants who owned small farms, making them property owners or enemies of the state. The class conflict proclaimed by *Das Kapital*, Marx's reprisal against German society, was claimed as the justification for the Russian Revolution by the Bolsheviks. The revolution resulted in the demise of the Russian nobility, the clergy of the Russian Orthodox Church, the Russian middle class, and Russian property owners.

For seventy years, the Soviet Union tried to make communism work. At the end of seventy years, they had a failed economy, and a failed state. The workers were impoverished and enslaved by communist commissars. The collective farms were wasteful and inefficient. A rich agricultural country, Russia was turned from an exporter of agricultural products into the bankrupt Soviet Union, suffering from endemic food shortages under communist rule.

A World Turned Upside Down

Under communist stewardship, Darwin's principle of survival of the fittest was turned upside down. The hardest working, most intelligent peasants and workers who saved and bought small farms and established businesses were slaughtered as capitalists. They were replaced by the less industrious, simple, and lazy who owned nothing. The less industrious became workers, managers, and supervisors of communist factories and collective farms. The theory of Karl Marx turned survival of the fittest into survival of the indigent, the indolent, and the simple survivors of the purges who became the people of the new Soviet Union.

The state-controlled economy of the Soviet Union produced shortages and poor-quality work under a regime of socialist terror. The terror was the product of the mass purges to eliminate property owners and any signs of resistance to the communist rule. Instead of producing a workers' paradise in which the workers owned the means of production, socialism created a country of impoverished workers under the control of a brutal police state.

During the same time, the Soviet Union was an impoverished police state-controlled by a Communist Party cadre who controlled everything; the United States was the wealthiest nation in the world. American workers enjoyed the highest standard of living anywhere in the world. Capitalism produced enough wealth to provide for the entire society, including the workers and farmers.

The American economy was managed by the invisible hand of supply and demand that proved highly efficient. Whereas the American economy was based on free enterprise, without state intervention, the Soviet economy was based on centralized state planning, state-imposed production quotas, five- year plans, and centrally directed distribution plans, all of which were the work of party managers. State planning was expensive, complicated, and inefficient, producing shortages, waste, and poverty. Comparison of the two systems, capitalism, and socialism, reveals that state planning and a socialist-controlled economy can't compete with free markets for effectiveness and efficiency.

Karl Marx got it wrong. Socialism was a failure. Whereas capitalism produced great wealth for both the workers and society, socialism produced inefficiency, poverty, and police state oppression. The results were clear. Capitalism created a more socially just society than socialism.

Marx got it upside down. It was the socialist state that stole from workers and enslaved them in a police state, not capitalism. Marx's socialist "workers' paradise" inverted Darwin's theory of evolution by killing off the most fit, while allowing the less fit to survive and operate centralized state planning, manage state-run factories, and operate state collective farms. The result of Soviet social engineering was survival of the least fit, poverty, a failed economy, and a bankrupt state.

Lenin's Theory of Colonial Exploitation

Lenin's denunciation of industrialized Western nations marked them as rogue nations guilty of criminal conduct. According to Lenin, the West had impoverished colonial countries to enrich their economies. Lenin asserted that the theft of the wealth of colonial countries increased wages, making workers in the West indifferent to Marx's call for class warfare. There was another explanation for the refusal of workers to revolt in accordance with Marx's theory (i.e., the theory was simply unreasonable). Why would well-paid German workers revolt? It was a possibility ignored by Lenin.

Just as Marx missed his mark, so Lenin also missed the mark. Lenin cited India, a colony of Great Britain, as his prime example of colonial exploitation. India was brought into the modern era by Great Britain, which built ports, highways, and railroads. India also received Western science, technology, self-governance, and democratic institutions from the British. The population was educated, and most important of all, India—a subcontinent of many separate ethnic groups and dialects—adopted the English language. English was taught in schools and spoken throughout India. English became the official language of government, business, and the arts, which permitted the country to assume its modern potential. In short, India prospered under British rule, but Lenin never admitted his error, although he lived to see India prosper under British rule.[19]

Indian prime minister Manmohan Singh spoke at Oxford University, refuting Lenin's charges. On behalf of the Indian people, he thanked the British for modernizing India, saying, "Today with the balance and perspective offered by the passage of time and the benefits of hindsight it is possible for the Indian Prime Minister to assert that India's experience with Britain had its beneficial consequences. Our notions of the rule of law, of constitutional government, of a free press, of a professional civil service, of modern universities and research laboratories have all been fashioned in the crucible where an old civilization met the dominant empire of the day."_[20] With these simple words, the Indian prime minister demolished Lenin's theory of colonialism—exploitation of colonial countries by the West.

Where Are We Today?

Progressive reformers launched a crusade to bring socialism to America in the late nineteenth-century. They embedded socialist teachings in their lessons, textbooks, and curricula. In so doing, they indoctrinated a large portion of the electorate with socialist philosophy that

---

[19] See Dinesh D'Souza, *America: Imagine a World without Her* (Washington: Regnery Publishing, 2014).
[20] *Ibid.*, p. 191.

condemns the American constitutional republic. Their disciples treat socialist beliefs as a secular religion. Together, they constitute a rival nation, or political culture, that seeks to overthrow the government and institute socialism. Progressive reformers have endangered public safety by alienating the American youth from their heritage for a cause that is destructive and false and will end in economic ruin.

Progressive reformers are domestic enemies of the USA. They should be dismissed from positions of responsibility in the academic community for fabricating history, advocating the overthrow of the government, and condemning the Constitution.

Our examination of Progressive reforms has surveyed socialist and communist political, social, and economic reform. Our review demonstrates that

- Karl Marx was wrong. Capitalism didn't steal from workers. Capitalism made American workers the wealthiest workers in the world.
- It is communism that steals the wages, the freedom, and the dignity of the workers in communist police states or dictatorships.
- Communism and socialism produce failed states and ruined economies.
- As Darwin's theory demonstrates the survival of the fittest, Marx's theory dictates liquidation of the industrious and the survival of the least fit.

Given the fallacy of the Marxist-Leninist theory, we must dismiss Progressive claims of theft of the workers' wages by American capitalists. Black students aren't victims of theft by Americans. They have no claim for compensation based on their standing as victims of capitalism. Consequently, we can justly assert that all lives matter. All men and women are created equal regardless of race, color, or creed.

Our examination of colonialism revealed that Lenin got it wrong. India prospered under British colonial rule. Thus, Lenin's claims of theft of the wealth of colonial countries by capitalism were wrong. On the contrary, the USA had acted as saviors for people of color. It was the nineteenth-century American capitalist society that freed the slaves at great cost in blood and treasure. It was the USA that insisted European countries give up their colonies at the end of World War II, bringing an end to colonial empires. Given the fallacy of Lenin's doctrine of colonial exploitation of third world countries by capitalism, radical black students in America are victims of neither capitalism nor neocolonialism.

Charges of American responsibility for slavery were false. It was English feudalism that established slave plantations in their colonies. It was English merchants and Arab slave traders who enslaved Africans and brought slaves to America. It was the English Crown and English landed gentry who established the slave plantations in the English colonies in America.

Members of society who consider themselves victims of slavery deserving compensation should take their demands to those who wronged them (i.e., the English Crown and the English landed gentry, who have been dead for centuries). To the extent black Americans have a claim against contemporary society for the sins of slavery, their complaint is not against the Union; it is against the Confederacy and the Democratic Party that profited from slavery and fought to preserve the institution of slavery in America.

Conclusions

The radical reformation of the American educational system to indoctrinate students with socialist doctrine constitutes sedition. The progressive reformers responsible are domestic enemies of the USA. The emergence of Black Lives Matter (BLM) is a direct result of the anti-American indoctrination of American youth by progressive educators.

BLM is a Marxist front organization created to wage revolutionary warfare. Their goals are to overthrow the American constitutional republic and to institute communism. BLM hides their radical goals by posing as a crusade against racial prejudice in America. As crusaders for social justice, they advocate the defunding of police departments and the closing of all prisons, which would leave their opposition in grave danger especially during an insurrection. They deny the high incarceration rate of black criminals is the result of the high crime rate of black criminals, which is absurd.

The operations of BLM encourage the assassination of police officers and exploit peaceful protests to stage violent riots that loot, burn and destroy commercial and private property. BLM is a dangerous terrorist organization that has captured the support of many well-intentioned but naïve young adults, especially professional athletes, who have unwittingly given their support to dangerous Marxist revolutionaries.

Chapter 8:

THE CONSTITUTIONAL REPUBLIC
VERSUS SOCIALISM

Five generations after Abraham Lincoln preserved the Union from the perils of rebellion, the Union is again challenged by a house divided. The Left demands fundamental change. They tell us that fundamental transformation of the American Republic is necessary to achieve social justice. We will examine the case for and against change.

We begin by looking at the principles that govern change. We will look at the character of the political parties by examination of their political philosophy and their record of governing. Examination of the principles of change plus the purpose of change, the methods of change and past performance should allow us to evaluate the case for and against change. Finally, we will draw conclusions from our examination of purpose, methods, and records of our political parties.

Principles of Change

"The end justifies the means" is an expression used to justify the use of force. Gen. William Tecumseh Sherman may have used the term to justify torching plantations and confiscating livestock and crops during his march to the sea. Sherman had previously told Gen. Ulysses S. Grant that a union victory was impossible until the breadbasket of the South had been destroyed. In Sherman's mind, Union victory justified the use of force to destroy the logistic base that sustained Confederate armies in the field. Confederates argued that Sherman employed evil means to achieve an evil end.

Whereas evil means produce evil ends, conversely, good means are necessary to achieve good ends. If we want our nation to be a model of liberty, equality, and justice—all noble ends—we need principled means that will create the noble ends we seek. In the final analysis, the character of the means employed shapes the character of the ends achieved. Regrettably, good intentions coupled with good means can be corrupted by incompetence; nevertheless, good ends are exclusively the work of good means well employed. The founders of the republic have held these principles and acted on them. Regrettably, they are often rejected by reformers holding alien philosophies.[21]

The American founding fathers dedicated their lives, their fortunes, and their sacred honor to liberty, equality, and freedom for all Americans. Seeking the blessings of the Almighty God, they commenced their quest for liberty in humble dedication of their lives to the greater good through principled means. Their work resulted in the Declaration of Independence, the Constitution for the new republic, and the birth of the United States of America. Principled means coupled with humble supplication for God's blessings yielded a rich harvest of ends that served as a model for representative government, wherein sovereignty rests with the people.

Confronting Change

Two centuries after the birth of the republic, much has changed. Discontent embitters those who reject American heritage, while resentful radicals reject the burdens of liberty and self-reliance. The most favored have turned from their spiritual roots and rejected the God of our fathers. The Constitution is challenged, and radical changes

---

[21] Saul Alinsky argues that evil means are necessary to attain communism. Alinsky teaches that the goal of the workers' paradise justifies all tactics and means necessary to destroy the American republic; lies, violence, character assassination, and class warfare are all legitimized by the ends of the Marxist revolutionaries. See Horowitz, Barack Obama's Rules for Revolution, p. 32.

to the political system are advocated by demonstrators. Slanderous attacks on the republic and its leaders constitute an undeclared civil war that rages in our midst. Every time our people vote in national elections, they are compelled to make far-reaching decisions that could fundamentally transform the republic.

The two political parties are very nearly opposites. At the risk of oversimplification, their agendas are described reflecting the unique character of the parties. Progressives seek fundamental transformation of America to achieve social democracy through income redistribution, socialized medicine, reduced spending for national defense, and big government to attend to the needs of the people, regulate the economy, and reduce pollution.

Conservatives seek to preserve American liberties, to defend the Constitution, and to encourage free enterprise. To achieve these ends, they seek to reduce the size of state and federal governments, to reduce the trade deficit and national debt, to build a strong national defense, and to grow the economy through the development of natural resources and lower taxes.

As we have observed, the means determine the character of the ends. The means chosen to attain the agendas of Progressives and Conservatives will determine the character of our republic. What means are to be employed by Progressives and Conservatives that will determine the character of the republic in the days ahead? Political beliefs, as well as previous conduct, provide indications of the means that will be employed. The Progressives and

Conservatives hold political beliefs that reflect different philosophies.

Progressive Philosophy

Progressives hold that man is a child of nature born unspoiled but corrupted by feudalism as taught by Jean-Jacques Rousseau. They hold the philosophy of European thinkers regarding secular humanism, the evolution of species, and the origin of the universe. They share the beliefs of Karl Marx, who has taught that modern man must break the chains of economic repression to build a socialist state in which the workers are the owners of the means of production.

Progressives embrace Lenin's rebuke of Western colonialism for stealing the wealth of their colonies. Progressives employ community organizers to recruit dissidents by exploiting local grievances. They believe the earth is endangered by pollution of the atmosphere, resulting in rising oceans. They embrace the theory of multiculturalism that teaches that black African tribal cultures are equal to the cultures of Greece and Rome. They espouse postmodernism that denies natural rights, tradition, and virtue as social constructs.

Progressives see capitalist societies as fundamentally flawed by a past exploiting slaves, women, workers, minorities, and colonial societies. They accuse America of exploiting slavery, colonialism, minorities, and women.

Progressives are secular humanist and socialist in outlook. They reject Western civilization as the work of corrupt capitalists. They seek restrictions on the use of fossil fuels to halt the shrinking of polar ice caps and the rising of the oceans. They seek to rewrite the Constitution to institutionalize Progressive reforms.

Conservative Philosophy

Conservatives embrace the Western civilization, the ethos of the founders and Abraham Lincoln. They generally believe that man is imperfect and born with original sin. They believe the Constitution should be interpreted as written by the founding fathers.

They seek to preserve liberty, expand opportunity, and achieve prosperity by liberating entrepreneurs from an excess of constraining regulations and by reducing the size of the federal government. They seek to stimulate economic growth by eliminating trade deficits and the national debt while reducing the burden of taxation on industry and private citizens. They hold that a strong national defense is essential to preserve the peace.

Accordingly, they seek to restore neglected and depleted armed forces. They view hysteria over melting ice caps as socialist justification to take control of industry and farming. They reject multiculturalism as a subversive theory that falsely denigrates American exceptionalism and discredits Western civilization. They reject postmodernism as an attack on moral values by amoral, radical dons.

Conservatives take great pride in American heritage, believing America is tolerant, open, and a force for good in the world. Whereas Progressives see America as fatally flawed, Conservatives see America as an example of a government by, for, and of the people that has brought liberty to our people, unprecedented opportunities to society, and unparalleled wealth to American workers. Moreover, Conservatives believe that America has made significant contributions to world peace. American armed forces have made major contributions during World War II by helping our allies defeat Nazi Germany, fascist Italy, and imperial Japan. In the postwar reconstruction, the United States has financed rebuilding the economies of Western Europe and forced European allies to give up their colonial holdings.

American deterrence of Soviet and Chinese communist aggression preserved peace during the Cold War. Contrary to the teachings of Lenin, the United States did not seek colonial holdings in World War II, Korea, Vietnam, Kosovo, Iraq, and Afghanistan. In each conflict, the United States fought to halt aggression and preserve peace at great cost in American lives and treasure. It is a rich history of selfless accomplishments denied by revisionist historians.

The Controversy over Slavery

What are we to make of Progressive charges regarding American responsibility for slavery? The English brought the first black African slaves to their colony in Virginia in 1609. It was the English Crown that put in place the system of plantation farming in the colonies based on slave labor. The English Crown established the mercantile system to maintain monopoly control of all trade with their colonies in America.

The Crown established a comprehensive commercial enterprise consisting of English law, English rule, English slave trade, plantation farming based on slave labor, and trade with the mother country.

Over time, the system became highly profitable except for the costs incurred protecting the colonies from foreign encroachments by the Spanish from Florida and by the French and their Indian allies along the western frontier. When the Crown attempted to raise taxes to pay expenses incurred during the French and Indian War, the colonies demurred. The English insisted on their right to raise taxes to pay for costs incurred defending their American colonies. The dispute occasioned the American Revolution, a bitter long war, and American independence.

When the English colonists in America drove out their English rulers, the colonies became independent states that formed the United States of America. Overnight, the former English colonists became American citizens who inherited a slave-based economy based primarily in the heavily agricultural South. Inasmuch as English colonial law remained in force in each of the former colonies, slavery was enforced by law. Accordingly, the United States became responsible for a population of three million destitute black slaves stripped of their African culture and unassimilated into American culture.

Americans were deeply conflicted by the ethical problem posed by human bondage. The founders could not abolish slavery, which would have ended the Union at a stroke of the pen, but they condemned slavery in the strongest possible language by declaring that all men are created equal. A great civil war would be necessary to remove the ethical contradiction posed by slavery—an unethical institution declared illegitimate by the founding fathers in their first official act announcing the birth of the nation.

Americans were not responsible for slavery. Americans did not legalize slavery inasmuch, as the institution of slavery was protected by law when the first Americans assumed positions of authority in the new republic. The English Crown established the slave trade and plantation slavery to enrich the Crown and the English landed gentry. When Americans took possession of the former English colonies in 1776, they became the owners of a slave-based economy that was the fruit of the sins of the English Crown and the English plantation owners. [22]Their sins were visited

---

[22] From the time of the introduction of African slaves in Virginia until the liberation of their decedents from the bondage of segregation in 1965 was 365 years—12 generations and 6 years.

on their sons and slaves in the form of slavery and segregation for more than twelve generations.

It was the sins visited on the sons and slaves that survived the revolution. The Southern planters recognized the language of the Declaration of Independence as an existential threat to their slave-based economy. The planters would lose their fortunes if the opponents of slavery enforced the nullification of slavery contained in the Declaration of Independence. Accordingly, planters united against regional and commercial interests opposed to slavery. Slave states joined together to maintain a balance of power in Congress to preclude legislation abolishing slavery.[23]

As the country expanded, new states were formed on the frontier. Settlers and legislators who opposed slavery challenged the authority of Southern planters to bring slaves into the new territories. The Missouri Compromise temporarily reduced tensions between North and South by ensuring that a balance of free and slave states was admitted to the Union. The compromise averted a crisis by preserving a balance of power in Congress that protected slavery and the financial interests of the planters.

Abraham Lincoln became the sixteenth President of the United States and the first Republican elected to the presidency.

---

[23] Despite the opposition of the planters, Congress outlawed the African slave trade in 1808.

He ran for office on a platform opposing slavery. Lincoln's victory in the elections of 1860 threatened the South with opposition to the institution of slavery vested in the highest office in the land. South Carolina succeeded from the Union in protest, which was followed a year later by the formation of the Confederacy. The succession of the South resulted in the Civil War. The Confederacy waged war to preserve states' rights and the institution of slavery. At a cost of 720,000 fatalities on both sides, countless casualties, and enormous treasure, the North won the war. The Union was preserved. The slaves were freed, and slavery was abolished by the Thirteenth Amendment to the Constitution.

The Thirteenth Amendment did not bring an end to the persecution of the former slaves. Segregation was introduced that denied people of color access to white only schools, sports, restaurants, and accommodations. Segregation denied black citizens rights that were protected by the Constitution. Their lost rights were not restored until passage of the historic Civil Rights Legislation of 1964.

Despite the long record of oppression by plantation owners and the Southern Democrats, contemporary Democrats are seen as the champions of black descendants of slavery in America.

The party of the Southern planters was the Democratic Party, which worked to preserve slavery in Congress before the Civil War. The Democrats waged the Civil War to preserve slavery. The Democrats introduced segregation to deny black citizens their civil rights. The Democratic Party opposed civil rights legislation abolishing segregation. This is the same Democratic Party that is seen today as the champions of black Americans.

How do the Democrats evade responsibility for their record of oppression of black Americans? Educators who support the Democratic Party are complicit in concealing the long history of black oppression by Democrats. They do it by teaching biased accounts of American history. They do it with the support of the liberal media, who conceal the dismal past of the Democratic Party. They get away with it because Republicans ignore the problem out of fear of being labeled racists.

In the post-segregation era, the descendants of the planters, who were religious believers, abandoned the Democratic Party, which no longer reflected their values. The Democrats had moved to the Left during the turbulent 1960s, adopting the popular values of the age. By the time civil rights legislation became law, the Democrats were waging class warfare while exploiting the grievances of class, gender, and race. While not all Democrats of the period were radicals, all the radicals were Democrats. The new Left—composed of Students for a Democratic Society (SDS), the Black Panthers, the National Organization for Women (NOW), the Vietnam Veterans Against the War (VVAW), and the Weathermen—was unacceptable to Southerners. The progenies of the planters were never Marxists, and they broke with the Democratic Party, which provided sanctuary for the new Left.

Attempting Cultural Suicide

The founders established the United States of America as a constitutional Republic dedicated to the service of Almighty God as part of the Judeo-Christian heritage of Western Civilizations. Their testimonials to faith in God are written upon the public building of the nation, upon the memorials to our leaders and on the majestic statues that celebrate our heroes. It is a rich heritage that survives to this day, but only in the conduct of religious worship and in public reenactments of traditional ceremonies. Prayer has been inappropriately removed from the classroom and the public square as a violation of the separation of church and state.[24]

The transition from one nation under God to the secular state was rooted in secular academic institutions that celebrated the French enlightenment as the birth of modernity. It was a gradual transition that occurred over time as American scholars returned from studies abroad and European philosophers gained greater recognition in America. During the administration of President Woodrow Wilson, it was publicly accepted that the founder's heritage was alien to the modern liberal views of the establishment. By the time Barack Obama became president, it was

---

[24] The constitutional protection of the separation of church and state was intended to prohibit the establishment of a state religion, as Henry VIII did with the establishment of the Anglican Church. It had nothing to do with school prayer or prayer in the public square.

fashionable to publicly declare that America was not a Christian country.

By the time Kingman Bruster declared the Vietnam War immoral in 1968, it was politically incorrect to teach Western Civilization in progressive academic institutions. The classics fell victim to politically correct doctrine that rejected capitalism, God, and the works of dead white males. Multiculturalism had replaced Western Civilization and American exceptionalism. Socialism had made free markets vulgar in the eyes of progressives. Classical literature was replaced by third world tracks complete with a Marxist emphasis that condemned capitalism and neo-colonialism.

A cultural revolution had occurred. It impoverished academic studies by banishing the majestic works of the greatest artists of the most advanced cultures that brought the world the enlightenment, the industrial revolution, modern technology, and the greatest music, prose, and poetry ever written. The classics were replaced by gender and ethnic studies in a metaphorical book burning as through as the Nazi book burning of the 1930s.

Progressive Means to
Fundamental Transformation

Turning from the survey of philosophy to the means toward ends, we look at the actions and activities employed by Progressive reformers to build a more perfect society. They teach that Democrats are apostles of change in the quest for a more perfect society. In so doing, Progressive educators inculcate positive images of Democrats, portraying themselves as virtuous citizens who sincerely care for the disadvantaged unlike Conservatives. They emphasize Progressive goals while they conceal the dismal past of the Democratic Party.

Progressives mask their past to conceal the long history of black oppression by Democrats. It is a deception that conceals their past from all Americans. It is a ploy that has been highly successful. Concealing the unethical past of the Democratic Party demonstrates the party has few scruples when it comes to waging the power struggle in America.

Accepting no responsibility for a disgraceful past, Democrats fault America for slavery as a corrupt capitalist society dominated by white patriarchs. By faulting America, Democrats vilify the heritage of the capitalist society they intend to eliminate while they defame white males. The defamation of white male property owners marks them as targets in the impending purge of property owners by socialists building the new social order.

Progressives build their base by exploiting local grievances by community organizers to mobilize opposition to the capitalist political system. It is a tactic employed by Lenin and Mao to build their revolutionary movements. It is the motive force behind identity politics. It is intended to build divisiveness, confrontation, and demands for radical change. By employing the revolutionary strategy of Lenin and Mao, they demonstrate their willingness to wage class, gender, and racial warfare in a sweeping power struggle.

Democrats use character assassination to silence debate on climate change. Academic freedom should permit open debate to allow the facts to speak for themselves. Assertions that the science of global warming is settled science means *We don't want to talk about it*, which is intellectually dishonest. Silencing debate, coupled with the enforcement of crippling regulations on industry, is an autocratic imposition of harsh emission standards never approved by the voters or their elected representatives in Congress. Substitution of intimidation and dishonesty for open and honest debate is an indicator that similar problems will be handled in a similar manner in future Democratic administrations. We can expect intimidation, dishonesty, and enforcement of regulations that impose unaffordable emission standards on American industry and workers.[25]

Democratic Party officials at the state and local level have enabled mobs to loot and burn communities in Ferguson, Missouri, Baltimore, Maryland, Minneapolis, Minnesota, Portland, Oregon, Kenosha, Wisconsin, and New York City. If not officially sanctioned race riots, they are racial disturbances permitted by local officials by looking the other way while restraining police officers from enforcing the law.

---

[25] See Matt Ridley, "Climate Coercion," National Review (November 19, 2015), pp. 55–57.

As a result of unpunished criminal behavior, local Democratic officials have emboldened black rioters, who act as if they are above the law. Their actions amount to class warfare enabling violent mobs to destroy middle-class businesses and properties.

Indifference to black criminal conduct by local officials and the media, coupled with intimidation of local law enforcement officials by the former Obama Department of Justice, has placed black offenders above the law. Protecting criminals by local authorities restrains law enforcement and places police officers at a greater risk.[26] Moreover, men and women serving in law enforcement see overt favoritism shown toward black criminals as racial bias that encourages conviction of law enforcement officers of criminal conduct.

During the 2016 political campaign for the presidency, Democrats serving in the federal bureaucracy (CIA, DOJ, FBI, NSA, and IRS) used the powers of the federal government to defeat political opponents and shield democrats from prosecution for breaking the law. It was an unprecedented misuse of federal resources created by Congress to protect the country from criminals and foreign antagonists.

Federal authority was misused to advance the agenda of the party in power. In so doing, political activists in the

---

[26] See Josh Gelernter, "Unhinged Hatred of the Police," *The Weekly Standard* (October 12, 2015), pp. 22–23.

Obama administration carried out a pattern of high crimes against the Constitution that was previously unheard of in the two hundred and forty years since the founding of the Republic.

Members of the FBI used Russian disinformation paid for by the Clinton campaign to justify spying on the Trump campaign. Known as the Steele Dossier, the Russian disinformation was also used to justify the appointment of a special counsel to investigate allegations of collusions with the Russians to rig the election by the Trump campaign. (It was an audacious political move that accused Trump of committing the dirty tricks used by Hillary Clinton, who had purchased disinformation from the Russians to destroy her GOP opponent.) The actions of the FBI agents were unlawful and done with full knowledge that the Steele Dossier had been paid for by the Clinton campaign and the charges were entirely bogus.

While aggressively attacking the GOP, federal employees loyal to the Clintons used their public offices to provide protection from prosecution for Democrats, who committed criminal offenses. The Democrat candidate for president was cleared of serious criminal charges that were substantiated by overwhelming evidence.

Multiple charges of violation of regulations governing the handling of classified information by the Democratic candidate were dismissed by the FBI Director as conduct that could not be prosecuted, as there was no intent to violate the law.

This determination was made even though proof of intent was not required to prove a violation of the federal regulations in question. The dismissal of the charges was a decision that showed complete disregard for the rule of law and the oath of office taken by FBI agents. This travesty of justice was reiterated when the DOJ later refused to charge the vice president and his family with accepting bribes from foreign powers, despite widespread evidence that serious crimes jeopardizing national security had been committed.

At the same time, over at the IRS, officials of the Obama administration denied tax exemptions to conservative advocacy groups, while tax exemptions for advocacy groups working for the Democrats were approved expeditiously. To further the discrimination being directed at conservatives, income tax audits were used to harass conservative Political Action groups (PAC) to handicap conservative fund-raising activities. Here again the powers of the federal government had been misused by the party in power to achieve a partisan political advantage.

It was another example of unscrupulous abuse of power by party activists working in the federal bureaucracy that previously had been unheard of throughout the history of the Republic.

The Pandemic

During the COVID-19 Pandemic of 2020 Democrat governors took advantage of the emergency to remove safeguards to prevent voter fraud and to impose severe restrictions on civil liberties in the name of public safety. The voting safeguards were abolished at the direction of state officials and judges, but not by the state legislatures that alone have the constitutional authority to determine how voting is to be conducted. The abolition of voter safeguards created a serious threat to democracy by opening the door to massive voter fraud.

The defeated GOP candidate in the 2020 presidential elections would later claim the election had been stolen by fraud on the part of election officials and civil servants managing the ballot count. The Supreme Court refused to hear the case that was based upon a breach of Constitutional Law. Despite having jurisdiction in the case, the Supreme Court denied a hearing on procedural grounds that gave the appearance of a denial of impartial justice by the Chief Justice, who refused to hear the case.

The Pandemic restrictions imposed on civil liberties changed the conditions that governed the daily lives of virtually all Americans. Citizens were told to shelter in place, wear masks in public, wash their hands frequently, and maintain a social distance of six feet while conducting essential business. To reduce the spread of the virus, schools were closed. In addition, businesses, restaurants, public parks, and beaches also were closed. Millions of workers could not go to work. Many lost their jobs due to the Pandemic restrictions imposed that forced thousands of businesses to permanently go out of business.

Throughout the Pandemic activities ruled non-essential (e.g., church and synagogue attendance) were prohibited. While religious worship was ruled non-essential activity, selling liquor and marijuana were ruled essential community activities, reflecting frankly anti- clerical views on the part of the authorities. Exceptions to the Pandemic restrictions also were made to allow activists to conduct peaceful demonstrations that routinely escalated into attacks on the police, riots, looting, and the destruction of property.

The Pandemic had allowed progressive authorities to use public safety as justification to wage class warfare. Double standards allowed demonstrators from Antifa and Black Lives Matter to assault the police and burn down businesses, while religious groups and small business owners remained quarantined in their homes. In retrospect, it is clear the Pandemic provided progressive authorities with openings to advance their socialist agenda.

The emergency provided the cover needed by progressive authorities to attack First Amendment rights as well as to give the green light to dissidents to use mob violence to carry-out attacks on the police and the middle-class.

The Pandemic allowed Democrat governors to strike down First Amendment freedoms with complete disregard for the highest law of the land. The Free Press that had been in the Democrats' camp since FDR's day silenced all criticism of Democrats, while conducting blistering attacks of Trump and his base. Free speech was attacked from the classroom to Hollywood and beyond to include social media where accounts of the GOP leadership were simply terminated.

The result was a holiday for apprentice revolutionaries. Freedom of assembly, which was denied ordinary Americans, was permitted for Antifa and Black Lives Matter who conducted massive demonstration with impunity. Rioters who attacked the police, burned public buildings and destroyed business were protected by Democrats who paid their bail and encouraged insurrections that raged from Seattle to Baltimore and from New York City to LA. The Pandemic became a time of violence and mayhem that raged all across America.

What can we expect when Progressives gain control of the White House and both houses of Congress? Given their history of concealing a dismal past, Democrats can be expected to abolish transparency in the government. Given their toleration of mob violence, we should expect a continuation of mob violence to wage class, gender, and racial warfare.

Climate change will continue to be a priority concern that will justify punitive regulatory standards that will close coal mines, restrict oil drilling, and impose emission standards that will undermine the auto industry. Law enforcement will again become a target for mob violence and cop killing to encourage class and racial warfare.

Given their philosophy, we should expect to see Democrats fundamentally transform the political system. The government will be expanded to take control of the economy, medical care, higher education, and expanded welfare. Class, gender, and racial warfare will culminate in the persecution of class enemies.

The purpose of the fundamental transformation of the republic is to form a socialist administration to replace the constitutional republic created by the founding fathers.

Having examined the purpose, methods, and record of the Democratic Party, the conclusions are clear. Demands by radicals for fundamental transformation of America to correct injustice are justification to overthrow the government by a united front of progressive, socialist, and communist cadre under the direction of the Democratic Party.

Conservative Means to Preserve the Republic

Conservatives see demands to fundamentally transform America in the name of social justice as an attempt to overthrow the government and abolish the Constitution. Conservatives will continue to support the Constitution as written by the founding fathers. They will seek to protect liberty by reducing the size of big government and ending the usurpation of legislative and judicial authority by governmental agencies. They will seek to achieve greater prosperity by reducing taxation, reducing the federal deficit, eliminating unfair trade practices, and restoring the manufacturing base of the economy. Republicans will reduce the regulatory burden on business, industry, and farming.

The Republicans will continue to open the party to all members of society. Republicans will seek transparency in government. They will restore confidence in the law enforcement community by supporting the men and women in the law enforcement community. They will seek institutional safeguards to preclude the federal bureaucracy from waging political warfare against political opponents as what has occurred in the IRS, FBI, CIA, NSC, and DOJ under the Obama administration.

They will rebuild the armed forces depleted by unilateral disarmament by the Obama administration. Republicans will seek to unify the country by building a society that provides for all its citizens. In short, the Republicans will return the republic to its historic position as a shining city on a hill as an example of a government by, for, and of the people.

The Fourth Estate

The founding fathers provided First Amendment protections for the press to guard against tyranny. They expected a distribution of political opinions among the free press that would facilitate the expression of all views. The founders expected the free press to report honestly and fairly, without playing favorites or slanting the news to favor one party over another. Thus, the free press is not free. They have obligations to meet the expectations of the founders to carry-out their responsibility to fairly and objectively report all the news without bias or favoritism.

As we now know, the mainstream media have become Progressives and allies of the Democratic Party. They are no longer fair and balanced in their reporting by suppressing news favorable to Conservatives, while making incessant attacks on the GOP administration using stories seen as fabricated narratives by many Americans. By their conduct that ignores the obligations of the free press, it is apparent that the fourth estate has gone into business for the Democratic Party.

Consequently, it can be said that the liberal media no longer meet the expectations of the founders for a free and independent press. We conclude that the liberal media are unworthy of the safeguards built into the Constitution for the protection of the free press because they are no longer a free and independent press. They have joined one side in the debate.

The mainstream media have become Progressives, who wage ideological warfare against the opponents of the Democratic Party. To the extent they have failed to meet their responsibilities, the fourth estate has become enemies of the republic they no longer serve. It is time for the fourth estate to take steps to moderate their unconstitutional behavior that endangers public safety.

Chapter 9:

THE ROOTS OF INTER-PARTY RIVALRY

Political parties have varied personalities and fascinating histories. They are guided by political beliefs that date back to the founders, larger-than-life figures from the distant past. American parties trace their origins back to Pres. Andrew Jackson, who formed the Democratic Party in 1828, and Republican president Abraham Lincoln, who saved the Union and emancipated the slaves. In the years after their founding, Democrats have moved to the left, whereas Republicans have preserved Lincoln's conservative understanding of the republic and the Constitution.

Both parties identify their legacy with modernization. Democrats hold the philosophical traditions of the French enlightenment, while Republicans hold the philosophy of the founding fathers. Contemporary historians recognize the French enlightenment as the origin of modern times. This perspective places Progressives solidly in the camp of modern political philosophers. It is a recognition of legitimacy as an agent of progressive change not extended to Conservatives by liberal historians.

Gertrude Himmelfarb challenges the attribution of modernity exclusively to the French Enlightenment. Himmelfarb gives us new perspectives for understanding the Enlightenment. She identifies three separate enlightenments defining three separate roads to modernity. Her sweeping analysis sheds new light on the behavior of political parties. Himmelfarb presents her findings in *The Roads to Modernity: The British, French, and American Enlightenments.*[27]

In addition to the French Enlightenment, Himmelfarb identifies the conservative British Enlightenment and the liberal American Enlightenment. Whereas Republicans have once been denied the imprimatur of modernity, Himmelfarb's analysis recognizes Republicans as agents of change. Himmelfarb's far-reaching analysis identifies the political philosophies of the British, the French, and the American Enlightenments.

Her work reveals the impact of political philosophy on political parties. More importantly, she documents the fundamentally different approaches to modernization of the two American political parties. We will summarize

---

[27] Gertrude Himmelfarb, *The Roads to Modernity: The British, French, and American Enlightenments* (New York, 2005), 284 pages.

Himmelfarb's analysis describing the three enlightenments.

The British Enlightenment

The British road to modernity is the product of a long struggle between the English monarchy and the landed gentry. From the Magna Carta in 1215 until the Glorious Revolution in 1688, the gentry gradually gained political power. In 1688, the Glorious Revolution established parliamentary rule that granted the landed gentry the right to rule Great Britain. The English Reformation opened additional roles for the landed gentry when the Church of England replaced Roman Catholic clergy with Englishmen educated in English colleges.

The British enlightenment saw a flowering of learning in universities and among intellectuals who created a body of philosophy that shaped scientific thinking and the conduct of the affairs of the government.

Englishmen in Parliament contributed to political thought. The power-sharing responsibilities of members of Parliament influenced English political philosophy that was pragmatic and tested by practical experience. Thus, British political reforms tended to be limited in scope and enacted over a long period.

Social reform in Great Britain was a shared responsibility of clergy, intellectuals, and government. Parliament enacted reforms to address problems associated with rapid social change introduced by the Industrial Revolution. The Anglican and the Methodist churches played an important role in alleviating poverty, as well as caring for the sick and elderly. The shared responsibility for leadership and governance produced social reforms that were the work of community leaders, the church, and Parliament. The history of shared responsibilities produced a British road to modernity consisting in gradual political change and a civic culture of parliamentary democracy.

The French Enlightenment

The French road to modernity was characterized by conflict and political repression that reflected deep divisions between the monarchy and the common people. For generations, the Bourbon monarchy ruled France, the most influential Continental power of the eighteenth century. Its authority rested on the military, the nobility, and the church. The nobility administered the state in the name of the king. The Roman Catholic Church administered and staffed French schools, hospitals, and charities.

The king opposed political change that challenged royal authority. The church was similarly resistant to change. The church was challenged by the Protestant Reformation. Opposition to the church among French intellectuals took the form of secularism, or denial of the legitimate authority of the Catholic Church. Together, the monarchy and the church maintained a monopoly of state power.

French intellectuals were confronted by a powerful monarchy that allowed them no meaningful role in the outdated regime. Excluded from power-sharing, French intellectuals became disaffected. They produced a body of literature opposing the monarchy and the church. Opposition to the Crown resulted in persecution of intellectuals, who went underground to escape imprisonment. French philosophy and literature of the era became known as the French Enlightenment, which called for the abolition of the prevailing political system—the French monarchy and the church.

France had accumulated massive debts waging the wars of Louis XIV, which created instability. When change came, it took the form of the French Revolution. The king, the nobility, and the clergy were sent to the guillotine. Members of the nobility able to escape fled the country. The monarchy and the church were abolished.

The nobility was outlawed, and their lands were confiscated. The French government was transformed from a repressive monarchy into an authoritarian dictatorship ruled by secular leaders based on principles of liberty, equality, and fraternity within a radically transformed civic culture.

The American Enlightenment

The American Enlightenment was built on a foundation of English heritage and common law. Americans considered themselves Englishmen. Like the English, they were deeply religious people. They saw themselves as freemen entitled to self-rule. Virtually all the founding fathers participated in colonial governments. Their passion for the rights of Englishmen resulted in rebellion when they were excluded from participation in a parliament that taxed them but refused to seat them as voting members.

Whereas the British Enlightenment was dedicated to political and social reforms, the American Enlightenment was committed to liberty—freedom from the perceived tyranny of the English Crown and Parliament. The American founding fathers set out to form a popularly elected republican government that would protect the liberty of the people. In the words of the founders, the people were created equal and endowed by their Creator with rights to life, liberty, and the pursuit of happiness.

The American founders debated the best form of government for the united colonies to avoid tyranny. After much debate that was carried in colonial newspapers, the founding fathers drafted a constitution that united the colonies under an elected representative government that protected religious worship. The collected newspaper articles capturing the philosophy of the founders was published as the Federalist.

The Constitution provided for a limited government composed of three coequal branches: executive, legislative, and judicial. The government was constrained by checks and balances to limit federal authority. The government of the republic consisted in shared powers between state and federal governments. The shared powers, limited authority, and checks and balances were intended to preserve the liberties of the people. The American enlightenment reflected the philosophy of freemen dedicated to liberty and determined to exercise self-government as a constitutional republic.

Himmelfarb's Vision

Gertrude Himmelfarb studied at Oxford University, where she was introduced to English political philosophy. It was the work of conservatives who had protected the property rights of the landed gentry from encroachment by the crown. As we have observed, the Glorious Revolution of 1688 gave birth to English Parliamentary rule that gave the landed gentry the power of the purse.

A century later, Parliamentary rule gave immunity to English society from the revolutionary fever of mob violence that engulfed Europe in the years following the French Revolution. The ideas of the French Enlightenment had spread across Europe by Napoleonic armies, where they took root in the universities. They were ideas that never spread across the English Channel. Radical French philosophy of social justice by mob violence and terror to redistribute wealth had no appeal to the English electorate that held the monarchy in check by the power of the purse.

Consequently, there was a vast difference between the political cultures that prevailed on the opposite side of the English Channel. To the south, the ideas of the French Enlightenment were dominant. To the north, the civic culture of British Parliamentary rule prevailed. Gertrude Himmelfarb's grasp of English philosophy gave her a profound appreciation of the separate roads to modernity that had been provided by the unique experiences of the British and American peoples.

She saw that the British and Americans had achieved modernity with no help from the French philosophers. Her grasp of the profound differences in the three unique roads to modernity allowed her to formulate a brilliant narrative that revealed the British and American Enlightenments to the modern world.

The Roads to Modernity

Gertrude Himmelfarb does not examine the character of the regimes formed after the roads to modernity. Nevertheless, the implications are clear. Explicit conclusions connecting the dots will assign blame by identifying those responsible for exterminating enemies of the state. Assigning responsibility for crimes against humanity could result in a backlash by the party implicated. Himmelfarb may have omitted explicit conclusions to avoid defenestration or similar retaliation. Be that as it may, Himmelfarb has left it for the reader to draw conclusions that are self-evident. We will recognize implications of Himmelfarb's assessment.

The roads to modernity have taken us to a variety of destinations. Some destinations have been liberal societies and republics. Other destinations have been authoritarian dictatorships. Comparing the three enlightenments, we observe that liberal governments are formed by freemen to preserve their freedom, whereas authoritarian dictatorships are formed by enslaved people to abolish tyranny and redistribute wealth. We observe that religious people are predisposed toward liberal societies that protect religious worship, whereas radicals are predisposed toward a secular regime and society.

In the case of the British enlightenment, landowners, clergy, and scientists formed a constitutional monarchy dedicated to the preservation of the rights of Englishmen. The French Enlightenment provided a road to modernity that led to the abolition of the old regime, the redistribution of wealth, and an authoritarian dictatorship. The American Enlightenment created a road to modernity that led to a constitutional republic dedicated to the preservation of liberty and a government of, for, and by the people.

The End of the Road

Using the model formulated by Gertrude Himmelfarb, we recognize three roads to modernity that lead to a constitutional monarchy, a constitutional republic, and an authoritarian dictatorship. Shifting our focus from the Enlightenment era to modern times, we recognize the Republican Party has been derived from the American Enlightenment as the party of Lincoln. The American Enlightenment has produced a liberal society, a constitutional republic, and a government of, for, and by the people. The Bill of Rights of the Constitution protects religious worship and the rights of citizenship. The free market of the liberal American society has become the home of capitalism that has produced great wealth, which we refer to as the American dream.

The Democratic Party is devoted to modernization after the road to modernity of the French Enlightenment. The legacy of the French Enlightenment is revolution, civil war, and dictatorship to abolish the old regime and redistribute wealth. Today the Democratic Party is acting in a way that is consistent with the legacy of the French Enlightenment by rejecting the constitutional order and refusing to recognize the legitimate transfer of power after an election while advocating resistance to overturn the election results.

It is radical political change that threatens the republic with revolution and civil war. The Democratic Party has taken the road to modernity that leads to authoritarian dictatorship. By adopting the philosophy of the French revolutionaries, it is fair to say that the Democrats have acquired the political DNA of French revolutionaries. Their road to modernity is the same one taken by Lenin and the Russian revolutionaries.

The reason Democrats act like Bolsheviks is that they are related. Both the Democrats and the Bolsheviks have the political DNA of French revolutionaries. It is a conclusion made transparent by Gertrude Himmelfarb's analysis of the roads to modernization. Mao, Ho, Pol Pot, and Castro all followed the same road to modernization used by the French. They all possessed the political DNA of French revolutionaries. They radically changed their society by building totalitarian dictatorships as called for by the French Enlightenment.

What's the Point?

The point is that at some future date when the Democrats have imposed their will by establishing an authoritarian dictatorship, white male property owners will find themselves awaiting execution by the secret police. In their final reflections, they should remember what Gertrude Himmelfarb has told them. Had they been paying attention and voting for representatives of Lincoln's own, not the "hate America" revolutionary crowd, their fate would have been very different. What were they thinking? Property owners are considered counterrevolutionaries by the radical Left, who have made no secret of their intention of waging class warfare to crush property owners.

Why the ethnic cleansing of white male property owners? The state can't redistribute wealth without taking from those who have and giving to those who don't. Since property owners possess the disposable wealth of the republic, they become enemies of the people, and their property becomes property of the state. The white male identity of the property owners marks them as counterrevolutionaries by identity politics. Enemies of the people are sentenced to slave labor if fit to work or shot, if not. Those are the rules observed by Lenin for disposal of enemies of the State.

Caveat

Intellectual elites of the liberal establishment act as if they alone have the right to select the president. They should read the Constitution. The people are sovereign in the American republic, not writers for the *Washington Post* or the *Weekly Standard*. Privileged journalists have one vote. Despite advanced degrees from exclusive colleges, their vote carries no more weight than the steelworker's vote or the coal miner's vote. While privileged journalists pontificate, America is in an existential struggle with Marxists, terrorists, globalists, and rogue states.

Defending the Constitution is essential to the survival of the republic. Survival takes the efforts of all patriotic

Americans to protect the last best hope of Western civilization. Dissenting critics calling themselves conservatives need to recognize the futility of rejecting the will of the American people. Negative resistance is counterproductive. They should roll up their sleeves and go to work with the people of the republic.

Chapter 10:

<u>WHAT TO MAKE OF FAKE NEWS?</u>

A heated dispute broke out in 2017 over accuracy of reporting that quickly became front page news. Social media experienced a flood of presidential messages denouncing fake news. The exchange became harsh after Donald J. Trump occupied the oval office, although GOP base secretly applauded the uproar.

The GOP had found a Commander-in-Chief who wasn't shy about taking on the liberal media. Dismayed journalists – unaccustomed to public ridicule from the bully pulpit – loudly rejected the fake news label. Pundits denounced Trump and his base as bigots – "deplorables" according to Secretary Clinton. Both sides saw themselves as blameless victims of shameless conduct.

The dispute was difficult to assess. We saw what appeared to be a standoff. Both sides stood by their stories. Despite strongly held opinions of all concerned, someone appeared to have been in the wrong. Nonetheless, despite outward appearances to the contrary, both sides may have been telling the truth. The counter-intuitive reality is that from a doctrinal perspective, both sides were on solid ground. They were telling the truth about different worlds seen through very different versions of history. The conflicting accounts of history are rooted in social change.

The Origin of Socialist Justice

The split between Western Civilization and socialist doctrine, specifically modern secular humanism, dates to the time of the French Revolution when French philosophers broke with traditional French culture. They had concluded the French social contract was unjust and unsustainable. They argued that the social conditions in France during the time of Louis XVI were so unjust that they had no right to exist.

They concluded a backward French regime that was fundamentally a feudal social order must go. They asserted French society must be radically reformed, rejecting God, Western Civilization, and the monarchy. The French philosophical counterculture created a body of literature we know as the French Enlightenment that is widely recognized as the beginning of modern times by contemporary historians.

The French Revolution destroyed the French monarchy, the clergy, and the French nobility creating a secular society governed by a revolutionary dictatorship. In the years following the French Revolution, the anti-feudal thinking of the French enlightenment was taken to a new level by the Marxist theory of class conflict that advocated the abolition of capitalism. Written by Karl Marx, a Nineteenth Century German philosopher, the anti-capitalist dogma created a new radical opposition to the establishment that called for the abolition of private property. The new doctrine appeared to complete the work begun by the French Revolutionaries and was promptly adopted by the radical left.

Marx maintained that capitalism creates class conflict. Marx explained that the industrialists who owned the factories were guilty of theft of their workers' wages. Marx called for a workers' revolution to liberate the people, who were oppressed by capitalism. The revolution in the name of the people would create a workers' dictatorship to abolish property owners creating a classless society. Theoretically, workers would own the means of production under the new social order. Marx called the end state of communist revolution a workers' paradise in which class conflict was supposedly eliminated.

In October 1917, the Bolsheviks carried out a coup that overthrew the Kerensky government starting the Russian Revolution creating a radical dictatorship that abolished capitalism. In so doing, the followers of Karl Marx and the followers of the French Enlightenment became the torch bearers of international socialism calling for a worldwide workers' revolution to build a more perfect world without class conflict. Contemporary socialists see themselves as disciples of Karl Marx, as prophets of social change to bring about more modern and just societies.

The Holiday from Bourgeois Morality

What were the practical consequences of adopting the secular humanism of the French Philosophers? *God is dead* becomes a central belief of the new social order. The primary restraint on personal behavior becomes preserving one's reputation as a French citizen as opposed to observing God's Law. The Ten Commandments become a Hebrew myth. It is permissible to lie, cheat or steal to advance the Party agenda.

Secular humanism and atheism are the guiding philosophies of communists, socialists, and fellow travelers. Atheism and secular humanism are a license to engage in formerly unethical behavior. In accordance with the teachings of Saul Alinsky, the preeminent American communist philosopher, atheism opens the door to new opportunities to gain the upper hand in the quest for political power.

In his book, *Rules for Radicals*, Alinsky tells how he partnered with Chicago mobsters to learn to make crime pay. Based upon his understanding of crime, Alinsky advanced socialism mobilizing mobsters, disgruntled laborers and unemployed roughnecks using false charges – wedge issues – to launch revolts against businesses and community leaders. By accusing reputable firms of heinous crimes, Alinsky demonstrated how amoral radicals could shake down the establishment. To illustrate his liberation from middle class morality, Alinsky recounts how he cheated cafeterias to eat without paying for his meals, while he was a student at the University of Chicago.

Advancing the Revolution

The worldwide socialist revolution didn't take-off as predicted by Karl Marx. The French revolutionaries and their comrades in the subsequent Russian Revolution did not bring the rest of the modern world with them in their quest for social justice. Others, like the English and the Americans went their own way. The English and the Americans had their own enlightenments that created liberal societies.

The English Enlightenment retained religious worship, private property, parliamentary rule, and the monarchy. The American Enlightenment retained private property, religious worship, and individual liberty under government by, for and of the people.

Among the many dramatic differences between communist and liberal societies, are the differences in the character of the civic cultures. Marxist societies rely upon secret police and para-military forces to engineer the new social order by force, what Mao called acquiring political power from the barrel of a gun. Purges of enemies of the people create a reign of terror, triggering the elimination of the middle class, the clergy, the nobility, and property owners. Annihilation of millions of souls is no small task. Slave labor, the Gulag, and concentration camps were essential tools used by Lenin to eliminate enemies of the Soviet Union.

Socialism Vs the American Constitution

Today the Democrats and the Republicans see the world through the lenses of very different experiences, values, and traditions. Progressives, socialists, and democrats see themselves as morally superior to conservatives by practicing a doctrine that advocates redistribution of wealth to eliminate poverty. The price is seldom mentioned as it entails a reign of terror to purge those wedded to ownership of property and religious worship. Whereas Democrats see themselves as agents of change, Republicans see themselves as conservatives preserving a rich past. They are the guardians of a constitutional order that has protected freedom and liberty since 1776 – more than eight generations.

President Trump's fake news is the politically correct edition of the daily news as reported by liberal journalists. As progressive reformers, they function like Eighteenth Century French philosophers coaching the common people to be insurrectionists. Their objective is to transform the loyalty of the people from support for the Flag to support for revolutionary change. They work to turn love of country into hatred of a corrupt political system that leaves the people in poverty, as predicted by Marx's theory of class conflict.

The Left undermines the old social order by trashing American heritage and denouncing religious faith. The sexual revolution of the 1960s was the work of progressive reformers, who advocated sexual liberation to corrupt the morality of the people. The left seeks to discredit America and rally support for revolutionary change. They claim the moral high ground as the "saviors" of the victims of American capitalism.

The criticism of the Commander-in-Chief by liberal journalists works to weaken the authority of the President, endangers US foreign policy and undermines the constitutional order. Whereas President Trump presents his administration in the best possible light, the Left attacks the legitimacy of the President and vilifies his agenda. While the President works to restore the economy, create fair trade and restore border security; the mainstream media fault the President for spoiling the environment and impoverishing foreign workers. Meanwhile Democrats in Congress have refused to fund the border wall, encouraged foreigners to cross the border illegally and impeached the President. In short, the radical Left has waged an undeclared war against the President and his agenda.

The bottom line is fake news is news that tells the story in terms of the values, beliefs, and traditions of those who report the story. In other words, fake news is typically authentic in the eyes of the writer. Despite the presumption of social justice of the cause by members of the socialist movement, including liberal journalists, they remain un-American liars, cheats, and thieves in the eyes of Donald J. Trump and his supporters.

Americans are split over who is at fault for fake news. Both sides accuse the other side of lying. Figuring out who is in the wrong remains too close to call for many Americans. However, there is no doubt about the fidelity of the radical critics of America. For American citizens to swear allegiance to foreign powers and the doctrine of Karl Marx betrays the Flag, the Republic, and the Constitution. Those who do so advocate the overthrow of the government and are guilty of treason.

As to the question of who takes the blame for fake news, agreement is nowhere in sight. Moreover, the question will remain unresolved until there is a final victory by one of the two adversaries in the socialist resistance and rebellion in America.

Chapter 11:

HONORING OLD GLORY

Our Judeo-Christian culture symbolizes America's foundation as part of Western Civilization. The English were charter members of Western Civilization, who passed their cultural heritage on to their colonies in America. The heritage of the West evolved from the faith of ancient cultures to become the heritage that unites Americans with the founding fathers of our Republic. The fidelity of contemporary Americans sustains the liberty made possible by the Republic through the Declaration of Independence. The freedom to practice our religious faith is essential to American heritage and is protected by the Bill of Rights.

What of the bonds of faith Americans have with the heritage of the founders? Do contemporary Americans retain the founders' belief that all men are created by God as equals? Devout Christians and Jews believe in a world created by God. They strongly believe in our right to full equality as children of God. They believe they are endowed by their Creator with inalienable rights to life, liberty, and the pursuit of happiness.

Whereas the faithful believe in God, secular humanists deny the existence of God and of life after death. The lack of faith of humanists challenges the bonds of faith between the founders and modern Americans. Such bonds are dependent upon the faith of informed citizens, *the people*, exercising free will to maintain our liberty and common heritage with the founders. Regrettably, their bonds of faith with the founders are threatened by politically correct (PC) gatekeepers of academia, who deny First Amendment rights and seek to abolish the Constitution.

Waging War against the West

Sir Isaac Newton observed that every action has an equal and opposite reaction. His scientific observations recognized the properties of matter. Newton's Law has a like application in philosophy as an analytical tool that teaches that for every thesis there is a response called an antithesis that presents an opposing view. Charismatic leaders and their teachings frequently generate an antithesis – a reaction contesting the original teachings.

Eighteenth Century French philosophers embraced atheism and rejected the French monarchy and culture – the antithesis of Western Civilization. Earlier opposition to the Catholic Church challenged questions of doctrine or abuses by members of the clergy. French philosophers called for a revolution to overthrow the monarchy and to abolish Christianity. The literature and thinking of the French philosophers are called the French Enlightenment that mobilized opposition to the Crown and triggered the French Revolution.

Over ensuing generations, followers of the French Enlightenment created a body of literature that called for fundamental reforms including the abolition of capitalism called for by Karl Marx in his seminal work on class conflict, *Das Kapital*. Marxist philosophy led to an uprising by the Bolsheviks that culminated in the Russian October Revolution of 1917 and the formation of the Soviet Union. Led by Vladimir Ilyich Lenin, the Bolsheviks called for the eradication of landowners, the institution of atheism as the state religion, and the elimination of capitalism.

Opponents of Western Civilization have waged war against societies that embrace Western culture. Their opposition stems from alien doctrines that cut them off from the rich heritage of the West. Such opposition includes militant religious groups as well as Marxist revolutionaries.

Whereas Marxist doctrine was published in the nineteenth century in opposition to capitalism, Islam was founded in the seventh century as a militant Bedouin religion. The followers of Islam were encouraged to carry out raids on neighboring tribes that were plundered and converted to the Muslim faith. Islam has retained its militant character over the centuries by continuing to observe their original doctrine that demands new conquests until all non-believers are converted to Islam.

Marxists and Muslims rejected the philosophy and learning of the West. To observe the rejection of Western culture at work within countercultures, one has only to observe the limited offerings in bookstores in Islamic states that strictly enforce Sharia Law such as Saudi Arabia. Arab literature is negligible, compared with English literature, consisting of works that meet the test of clerical censorship. Under Sharia Law publications that fail to acclaim Islam and reflect the teachings of the Koran are strictly forbidden. Marxists practice similarly strict rules of censorship.

Climate change is an example of an attack of the West that is misrepresented in America for political purposes. Climate change, an attack on the West by the socialist Left, was originally established as a racket to extort reparations for colonialism from the industrialized countries of the West by Third World nations. The United States, a former colony, should not be paying for the sins of European colonial empires. The Democrats agreed to pay the lion's share of the reparations for colonialism because the Left hates the USA and seeks to punish the American middle class (deplorables) for their religious faith and patriotism.

Evolution of Civic Culture

Civic cultures are many reflecting local customs and cultural borrowing during the evolution of civilization. Western Civilization evolved over thousands of years from the melding of Judeo-Christian culture with the learning of ancient Greece and Rome, that was capped by the scientific learning of Western Europe from the Middle Ages through modern times.

The British, French, and American Enlightenments gave rise to modern nation states, while developing modern civic cultures, including constitutional monarchies, constitutional republics, and totalitarian dictatorships. The constitutional orders were formed by free men to protect their liberty and rights. The totalitarian dictatorships were formed by enslaved people to thwart tyranny, to abolish the earlier culture and to redistribute the wealth of the society.

Western Civilization produced the most advanced cultures in history. It has produced countless masterpieces in music, literature, and art, while creating modern science and technology. The learning of Western Civilization created the British, French, and American Enlightenments, as well as the industrial revolution. Contrary to the doctrine of multiculturalism, the learning of Western Civilization has long surpassed that of third world cultures through the growth of learning among the world's best educated people and most prolific cultures.

As we have observed, Western Civilization produced an anthesis in the form of countercultures rejecting the religious doctrines common to the English and American Enlightenments. The rejection reflects the denial of Judeo-Christian culture, as well as Western Civilization. Islam rejects Judeo- Christian culture, whereas Marxist revolutionaries reject capitalism and Western Civilization. Both movements have waged wars to convert non-believers and destroy those who reject their doctrines – the anthesis of Western culture.

Despite the doctrinal denial of Western culture, the people of countercultures expose the foolishness of multiculturalism by voting with their feet. Even though multiculturalism teaches that all cultures are equal, the people of countercultures seek to adopt the learning of West. They send their children to be educated in the West. People constrained by the clergy of Islamic police states would not risk retribution to acquire Western learning, if all cultures were equal – an absurd doctrine advanced by intolerant, progressive educators to disparage Western Civilization.

Figure 3 is a Venn diagram depicting evolutionary cross-fertilization that produced modern liberal societies and their constitutional orders, as well as the principal countercultures rejecting Western Civilization. The doctrines of countercultures spread opposition to Western Civilization. Despite the claims of PC disciples of the New Left, there is no end in sight to the bloody conflicts waged by countercultures.

Extending Tolerance to Alien Cultures

Progressives preach tolerance of those holding beliefs alien to Western Civilization. The tolerance advocated by Progressives is a one-way street. Whereas Marxist and Muslim disciples exploit the tolerance enjoyed in liberal societies to spread their doctrines, they extend no such tolerance to Westerners residing in their communities – authoritarian police states.

Despite PC nostrums, doctrine dictates behavior. The doctrines of alien cultures wed Marxists and Islamic revolutionaries in opposition to Western Civilization. Their alien doctrines decree violent clashes with capitalists and infidels. Their followers wage class and religious wars against Judeo-Christian societies. The West didn't create the alien doctrines. Moreover, the West cannot unilaterally end conflicts started by our adversaries, despite misguided efforts to do so by the Obama administration. Consequently, there is no end in sight to the bloody cultural conflicts of our times, despite PC demands for tolerance that have no effect upon our adversaries.

In addition to the cultural differences between the West and alien cultures, cognitive variances differentiate the people of Western societies. Fundamental beliefs separate the globalist from the nationalist. Expectations separate establishment elites from middle- class citizens seeking jobs and economic growth. Doctrinal differences create clashes between socialist radicals on college campuses and students expressing conservative views. Religious differences among the faithful create internal dissonance as well. These differences are the price we pay for our priceless liberty that characterizes liberal societies. Despite such internal differences, national solidarity remains essential to preserve Western Civilization.

The religious Faith of Our Fathers serves as a unifying force within our society, however secular humanists reject religious faith disarming liberal progressives. Moreover, followers of countercultures in the West serve to undermine Western Civilization. Thus, the knowledge that defines us also separates us, presenting unique challenges in the face of serious cultural challenges. From a conservative perspective, loyal citizens should stand for the national anthem, embrace the faith of our founding fathers, and protect and defend the Constitution.

Honoring America

Honoring America by standing during the playing of the national anthem shows respect for the Flag. As American citizens *we pledge allegiance to the Flag of the United States of America and to the Republic for which it stands, one nation under God, indivisible with liberty and justice for all.* The pledge of allegiance is our social contract with our fellow Americans to protect the Constitution in spiritual union with those who established our heritage, built our country, and gave their lives in defense of Freedom.

Athletes who kneel during the playing of the national anthem are saying, "We reject your flag, your Republic, and your social contract." They are taking advantage of public displays of patriotism to demonstrate their commitment to a counterculture that seeks to abolish the Constitution. Their public displays of disrespect serve as an example for impressionable fans, thereby sowing the seeds of discontent within our diverse communities.

The right to the privilege of citizenship is nullified by rejection of the social contract that binds Americans together in defense of life, liberty, and the pursuit of happiness. For those who kneel in solidarity with revolutionaries, a reminder of the meaning of their actions is in order. Their brazen behavior nullifies their bond with American citizens. Accordingly, we must explain that the price of citizenship includes allegiance to the Flag and to the Republic for which it stands.

To protect the Constitution, Americans must reform our corrupt educational system to eliminate the socialist indoctrination that passes for education and vilifies our heritage. Progressive educators have abused their authority by trashing our heritage, alienating our youth, and threatening the Constitution. The Constitution that protects the rights of American citizens was never intended to shield traitors, who seek to destroy our Republic. Misuse of academic freedom to advocate the overthrow of the government is sedition. Academic freedom is not a permission to commit treason.

No one is permitted to destroy America and its sacred heritage. The treasonous intent of revolutionaries separates them from our common culture and American citizenship. We are bound by a social contract to support and defend the Constitution, not to provide sanctuary for revolutionaries determined to destroy our constitutional Republic.

Americans stand for the national anthem. Traitors take a knee. These traitors seek to fundamentally change America by adopting alien doctrines to include socialism. They include multiple front organizations such as Antifa, National Organization of Women and Black Lives Matter. They pose an existential threat to our constitutional Republic in a crisis as dangerous as any crisis since Abraham Lincoln was president. How many dedicated cops and innocent martyrs must be slain before Americans find the courage to confront our adversaries and defend the Constitution? Whatever the cost, patriotic Americans must stand firm in defense of what Lincoln called... *the last best hope of man*.

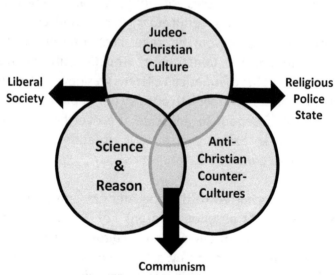

Figure 3: The Evolution of Civic Cultures

Chapter 12:

SURVIVORS OF THE KILLING FIELDS

Horrific experiences cause post-traumatic stress disorder (PTSD)[28] The victims differ widely. Nurses caring for severely wounded casualties often suffer from PTSD, as do emergency medical treatment specialists with a long history of caring for accident victims. Rape victims experience symptoms of PTSD as do survivors of disasters such as the crash of civilian airliners. And some, but not all, combat veterans return from war with symptoms of PTSD. The condition is viewed as a curse with no redeeming qualities, a judgment that is too harsh.

I cannot speak for all victims of PTSD. I can speak of the disorder experienced by combat veterans, which I share. I volunteered for and served two tours of duty and five campaigns in the Republic of Vietnam as a combat

---

[28] While not a product of Progressive reform, PTSD was recognized as a social problem during the era of reform.

infantryman and as a cavalryman. I was decorated for valor five times and was awarded the Purple Heart. I would have volunteered for more combat duty, but I was obliged to take an assignment in Germany to avoid a divorce._[29]

In addition to battlefield experiences that first brought me into contact with PTSD, I met officers and senior noncommissioned officers with PTSD while participating in group therapy. [30]The group therapy sessions were conducted by the Department of Veterans Affairs (VA). From experiences and observations of a lifetime, we recognized that PTSD can be helpful during combat operations.

For combatants exposed to repeated combat actions, PTSD arrives in the form of desensitized senses and suppressed emotions. These responses harden fighters and eliminate fear—a blessing that sustains combatants in tough times. After many months of combat duty, I experienced a loss of all emotions that was a blessing during combat actions, although I had no idea at the time that I was experiencing symptoms of PTSD.

PTSD is an emotional disorder caused by suppression of memories and emotions. It is the product of unconscious decisions to block horrific memories, to shed no tears, and to reject emotions that simply get in the way when combat requires a clear head. Stuffing our memories and emotions,

---

[29] I served thirty years in the army in infantry, cavalry, and armor assignments.

[30] These were professional soldiers. They had distinguished service records. Their symptoms of PTSD surfaced twenty years or more after their first combat duty.

not once but many times, buries our capacity for feeling emotions beyond recall. Combat veterans with many campaigns who have stuffed emotions for years have no visible emotions.

The same suppression of emotions is true for army and navy nurses serving in forward aid stations. They are routinely exposed to severely injured casualties with wounds that will normally produce grief or shock. Unfortunately, emotional displays will alarm patients. Consequently, nurses hide their emotions when caring for patients. Suppressing their emotions over many years leads to PTSD symptoms later in life. Nurses coping with PTSD have shared that their most difficult emotions are associated with the loss of severely wounded patients after long struggles to save the lives of brave young men and women.

Adapting to High Stress

Soldiers exposed to combat over many years become typical warriors. Having stuffed anxiety beyond recall over years, they become fearless. At the first sign of battle, they become calm, often eager to fight. Typically, combatants later diagnosed with PTSD are cool in battle, the natural leaders in the unit who thrive on combat. They kill to avenge fallen comrades and for the excitement of combat.[31] PTSD is their blessing in battle because it suppresses feelings, equipping them to be highly effective leaders. The cool head in times of great danger is a prince among men.

History records fearless warriors who have become legends in their time. Classical warriors demonstrated military virtue typically found in the Greek phalanx, Roman legions, and the ranks of Norman conquerors. Such were the Sergeant Yorks and the "Audie Murphys" of World Wars I and II who wasted enemy soldiers like no one else in their ranks. They may well have suppressed their emotions to get through killing that protected their buddies from harm. Did they have PTSD? Audie Murphy's biography revealed he was plagued by depression and memories of violent combat later in life.[32] Obviously, PTSD served him well in combat.

Returning Home

Nothing we do in a normal social environment compares to the violent killing of the enemy in close combat. When killers long habituated to the excitement of battle return from war, they don't fit in, and they don't know why. As warriors, they have adapted too well to the heat of battle.

---

[31] As General Lee said at the Battle of Fredericksburg, "It is well that war is so terrible, or we would grow too fond of it."

[32] David A. Smith, *The Price of Valor: The Life of Audie Murphy, America's Most Decorated Hero of World War II* (Washington, DC: Regnery History), 241 pages.

The qualities that steeled hardened warriors in battle have left them poorly equipped to rejoin society. Insensitive to suffering, indifferent to emotions, and still thirsting for the thrill experienced in the heat of battle, soldiers return home to find themselves stranded in a starkly different world, unable to relate to the privileged living lives sheltered from the violence of war.

They carry their battle-hardened character with them when they return from war. The battle-hardened character is coarsened by brutal combat environments in which combatants become oblivious to pain, insensitive to death, and embittered by the loss of close companions. Their combat experiences change the way they handle emotions.

Hypervigilance stamps their persona, as well as anger born of the mutilation and deaths of their buddies. As parents, they often lose the capacity to nurture children. As lovers, they may become cold and distant. As companions, they become divorced from the ebb and flow of everyday life. Generally, they lose the capacity to relate to the mundane preoccupations of polite society.

PTSD becomes a problem in civilian communities where it is considered offensive by those deferred from military service.[33] Animosity toward veterans has resulted in

---

[33] Victor Davis Hanson records the hubris in academic circles that assume war is bad and can be banished by morally superior beings who reject it. Such groups are intolerant of those who wage our wars and cope with PTSD. See *The Father of Us All: War and History, Ancient, and Modern* (Bloomsbury Press, 2010).

rejection of attempts to find employment when my generation has returned from war. It is a problem that hinders veterans from finding constructive roles in society.[34] Regrettably, society doesn't recognize that PTSD doesn't make the brilliant stupid or the problem solver irrational. On the contrary, it garbles their gifts with dysfunctional behavior, which is a problem that can be treated by the VA.

Treatment of PTSD

Those suffering from PTSD symptoms are frequently unaware they have PTSD. The PTSD carrier is often in denial about dysfunctional behavior—anger, emotional outbursts, and shut-down emotions. Others may realize they have a problem but don't know how to cope with emotions that spiral out of control. Regrettably, among the veterans who recognize they have emotional problems, many reject professional help because of the stigma attached to the treatment of emotional problems.

Denial is problematic because it closes the door to professional help. Those rejecting help often self-medicate with drugs and alcohol to cope with the symptoms of PTSD. Professional help allows them to understand their problems and receive medication to calm the warrior's

---

[34] After two years looking for work, I found work as a contract worker for the army in the Middle East, where I worked for ten years.

rage. Making the adjustments needed to cope with disabilities is important for survival.[35]

The VA is uniquely equipped to provide counseling and treatment for veterans coping with PTSD, which is the recommended solution to the problem. I offer my observations as one who has been there and done that every step of the way in a lifetime of embracing PTSD's blessings in combat, experiencing inappropriate defense mechanisms, denying disruptive behavior, followed by discovery and subsequent VA treatment and care.

Regrettably, we can't undo mistakes. The best we can do is to own our mistakes and share the hard-earned wisdom gleaned over a lifetime of service. I extend my heartfelt thanks to the VA medical staff and my fellow veterans who have made it possible for me to understand our failures and share observations. I count the VA staff and fellow veterans as trusted comrades with whom I have shared the difficult memories suppressed in combat. Their care, advice, and assistance have made it possible to resume a role in society, although it remains a very private role as an elderly disabled veteran.

Fearless leadership is a battlefield blessing that accompanies battle-hardened warriors by virtue of their violent past. Battle-hardened warriors are "habituated to combat" as Maj. Gen. George S. Patton described a

---

[35] Of those diagnosed with PTSD, the death rate for all causes is twice that of veterans not diagnosed with PTSD. See "PTSD Is Bad for your Health," appearing in the August 2015 edition of *VFW* magazine.

Vietnamese Rangers battalion commander who had spent his entire adult life at war. Did he and his men have PTSD? We don't know, but surely, some in their ranks have shared characteristics we know as PTSD, an unsung blessing in the heat of battle for those called on to act as leaders in combat.

Chapter 13

RED FLAGS

The years following World War II saw the expansion of the Soviet sphere of influence and the rise to power of the People's Republic of China. The Soviet acquisition of power over Eastern Europe was mirrored by the expansion of Chinese Communist power in Asia. Western interests in Asia were tested by a series of conflicts including the North Korean invasion of South Korea resulting in a brutal conflict ending in stalemate. Formosa was threatened by the People's Liberation Army, and Malaysia became the target of a long and ugly insurgency. Both nations were severely tested, yet both preserved their independence. The subsequent Vietnam War saw an embarrassing defeat for People's War, that nevertheless ended in the defeat of South Vietnam by the People's Army of Vietnam (PAVN).

The alliance of Western democracies resisting the export of communism by armed conflict gave us the North Atlantic

Treaty Organization and the South East Asian Treaty Organization. Both alliances provided barriers that contained communist armies from marching through neighboring countries. The era was characterized by Cold War, efforts to test containment, and covert conflict that tested the solidarity of the West. Covert operations were conducted by both the East and West in pursuit of security objectives through covert means. Clandestine conflicts were fought in secrecy to protect the homeland from clandestine threats and safeguard the hidden warriors who gathered vital intelligence.

The covert operations were highly classified. Many remain classified today, several generations after the clandestine clashes commenced. In the shadows of an extraordinarily complex period of history, much remains unexplained including covert victories and defeats. Some authorities refer to these mysteries as conspiracy theories which discredits the people, and the events involved. For the purpose of our discussion, we will call such mysteries Red Flags, meaning covert conflicts that cannot be explained by information within the public domain.

Before we close the book on American experience with communist revolutionary warfare, we will briefly address some Red Flag ambiguities that may have been the work of Lenin, Mao, Castro, and their secret comrades in the revolutionary wars of our time. They remain Red Flags for historians and students of the art of war. Principal Red Flag controversies include the Kennedy assassination, the 9/11 disaster that destroyed the World Trade Center, and the mystery surrounding the WMD of Sadden Hussein that triggered a war but their disposal by the US was never recognized by the Left. The information in each case is contested or incomplete, nevertheless the involvement of Soviet, Chinese Communists, or Cuban intelligence services is highly probable. Consequently, they are relevant to our study of Marxist revolutionary warfare. We do not know all the answers. We will look at what we do know, at what is alleged to have happened, and at the implications of the controversies.

The Kennedy Assassination

President John F. Kennedy was assassinated in Dallas, Texas at 12:30 p.m. on 22 November 1963. The President was riding in an open car in a motorcade. The assassin fired three shots from a window of the Texas School Book Depository. The President was hit and mortally wounded. Police made two attempts to arrest the suspect, Lee Harvey Oswald. The first attempt failed when the arresting officer was shot and killed by Oswald. A second attempt to arrest Oswald resulted in his apprehension. He was incarcerated in the Dallas County Jail. He was charged with the murder of the President at 1:30 a.m. on 23 November. In a bizarre turn of events, Oswald was shot and killed the next day by Jack Ruby.

The Kennedy assassination created an unstable and potentially dangerous situation. President Kennedy had been an exceedingly popular President. The emotional outpouring upon his assassination was heartfelt. People from every walk of life were deeply grieved by the President's murder. They were also angry. There was talk of retribution against those behind the murder plot. The initial evidence suggested that the Soviet Union could have played a role in killing the popular American President.

The newly sworn in President, Lindon B. Johnson and senior officials in his administration were concerned about the possibility of the escalation of a highly charged situation that could get out of hand. No one wanted World War III to be triggered by unchecked emotions, as occurred prior to the Spanish American War. Nether the US nor the Soviet Union wanted a nuclear war.

What were the facts? Lee Harvey Oswald, the assassin, was now dead, He was murdered in the Dallas County Jail by an outraged citizen, who took matters into his own hands. Because of Oswald's murder Intelligence officials were denied the opportunity to question Oswald to determine his motives or the possible involvement of foreign nationals in a plot to kill the President. What do we know about Oswald?

Lee Harvey Oswald had a history of disciplinary problems. He quit high school and joined the Marines in October 1956. While on active duty, he advocated radical Marxist theories that got him in hot water with the Marine Corps. He received a hardship discharge from the Marines in September 1959. Nine days later he left for the Soviet Union where he requested Soviet citizenship. He was assigned to work in Minsk, where he met Marina. They were married in April 1961. Thirteen months later he returned to the United States with his wife Marina. They resided in New Orleans, where Oswald formed the Fair Play for Cuba Committee and circulated Cuban propaganda. He traveled to Mexico City where he attempted to obtain a visa to visit Cuba but was denied.

Oswald moved on to Dallas where he found employment at the Texas School Book Depository. It was from a window in the Book Depository that Lee Harvey Oswald observed the motorcade of the President. A trained sharpshooter, Oswald took aim with a high-powered rifle. Firing three rounds Oswald hit the President inflicting mortal wounds. In so doing Oswald implicated the Soviet Union that had provided him asylum and employment. His ties to Cuba through the Fair Play for Cuba Committee also aroused suspicions that he may have been acting on behalf of Fidel Castro.

Incidents such as assassinations are laden with complications. Heads of state understood the seriousness of the incident. It was the assassination of the Austrian Crown Prince and heir apparent of Emperor Franz Joseph of the Austrian Hungarian Empire that had triggered World War I. Murdering a head of state could start a war with great suffering and loss of life. Oswald's ties to the Soviet Union and Cuba were problematic. They provided the appearance of foreign involvement in the assassination, a potentially dangerous history that could trigger a crisis. It was to examine the evidence and render recommendations that President Johnson appointed the Warren Commission to investigate the assassination of President Kennedy. The Warren Commission found that the President had been killed by a lone gunman and that there was no foreign involvement in the assassination of the President.

The Warren Commission Report

The Warren Commission Report had the desired effect that LBJ and his National Security Council were after. The crisis passed, passions cooled and a nuclear war with the Soviet Union was precluded. But the Report failed to convince the public that a lone gunman assassinated the President. The words of the authors were not sufficient to put to rest all the questions raised by the terrible events. Evidence existed that challenged the findings of the Warren Commission. Many years after the assassination we are unable to answer important questions. The following questions should have been more fully addressed:

1. How do we explain the evidence that suggests Oswald had the help of a second marksman?

2. How do we know Oswald was not part of a team sent by Castro or the Soviet Union to murder the President?

3. Was Jack Ruby acting on behalf of the Soviet Union by killing Oswald before he revealed information that implicated the Soviet Union?

Regrettably, we still do not know the answers. What we do know is the anxiety created by the Kennedy assassination has never been put to rest. It took seventeen years to start an independent investigation after the publication of the Warren Commission Report failed to convince the public that a lone gunman assassinated the President. The Warren Commission Report found that Oswald had smuggled the rifle into the Texas School Book Depository on the morning of the assassination in a brown paper package, which he had told a co-worker contained curtain rods. The conclusion that a conspiracy was involved in Kennedy's assassination was the assumption of those who studied the evidence and rejected the official lone gunman account.

Skeptics have argued that expert marksmen could not duplicate Oswald's shooting. To validate the lone gunman conclusion of the Report, tests were conducted by the Warren Commission (1964) and CBS (1967). In those tests, the marksmen attempted to hit the target three times within 5.6 seconds, which was the overall shooting time that was recorded on newsreels of the motorcade. Many of CBS's eleven volunteer marksmen were able to hit the test target twice in under the time allowed. None hit the target three times in 5.6 seconds. Either there was a second gunman, or Oswald's Marine Corps marksmanship training made it possible for him to accomplish what the marksmen were unable to do during the tests.

Speculation about the Kennedy assassination continues to this day. The failure of the Warren Commission Report to persuade suggests an official cover-up, which leaves open the possibility of foreign involvement in the Kennedy assassination. Despite the shortcomings of the report, the results achieved cannot be overlooked. War with the USSR was avoided in an extremely dangerous moment of history. Notwithstanding public dissatisfaction with the findings, the report has served the best interests of the American people by defusing a dangerous situation.

Destruction of the World Trade Center

Before 9/11, terrorism was not seen as a major problem in America. It was somebody else's problem. The average American had never felt the horrors of a terrorist attack. After 9/11, America had been ravaged by an attack that inflicted more death and destruction than the Japanese attack on Pearl Harbor on 7 December 1941. America's enemies had dramatically escalated the damage of their terrorist attacks and Americans demanded retribution.

The destruction of the World Trade Center on 11 September 2001 was a turning point in the war against terrorism. Before 9/11, terrorism was considered a threat to public safety. Terrorist acts were treated as a criminal offence to be handled by the criminal justice system. Terrorism was not seen as a serious threat to national security. After 9/11 Americans recognized Islamic terrorism as an existential threat to the nation. It was an act of war. Americans demanded a serious response to bring those responsible to justice. Following the 9/11 attack, American leadership had a mandate to seek and destroy those who carried out the attacks.

Who could have been motivated to carry out the attacks that destroyed the World Trade Center? With the downfall of the Soviet Union in 1991, a former enemy was no longer a communist power. Russia was seeking American aid. It was no longer a primary enemy of the United States and an unlikely suspect to carry out the attacks. However, Cuban intelligence was motivated and capable of carrying out such an attack. The American supported Bay of Pigs invasion of Cuba, as well as the American intervention to eliminate Cuban revolutionaries working to create an insurrection in Bolivia were seen as reasons to seek retribution. The CIA had killed Che Guevara in the process of wiping out the Bolivian rebels. What better way for Castro to even the score than to murder the popular American President?

What about US enemies in the Middle East? The Saudi nationality of the Arab terrorists, who carried out the attacks, was beyond dispute, which implicated Islamic terrorist groups operating in the Middle East. Islamic terrorists had been carrying out attacks on US embassies, American military facilities, and commercial airliners for years. Thus, Arab terrorist groups such as al Qaeda were primary suspects.

On September 11, 2001, nineteen Arab militants associated with the al Qaeda Islamic extremist group hijacked four airplanes and carried out suicide attacks against targets in the United States. Two of the planes were flown into the twin towers of the World Trade Center in New York City. A third plane hit the Pentagon just outside Washington, D.C. The fourth plane crashed in a field outside Shanksville, Pennsylvania. Almost 3,000 people were killed during the 9/11 terrorist attacks, which triggered major U.S. initiatives and reforms to combat terrorism that defined the presidency of George W. Bush.

At the time, 9/11 was the single most devastating attack on U.S. soil since Pearl Harbor. The reforms have included a reorganization of homeland security, a redefinition of intelligence collection responsibilities, as well as new guidance for the dissemination of intelligence. Rather than a competition to see which agency could scoop the others in intelligence collection, the purpose of intelligence collection was defined as a collaborative effort of a unified intelligence collection effort. Accordingly, new intelligence collection guidance was issued, and intelligence activities were placed under the direction of a single director.

Allegations of an Inside Job

Some observers believed the attack could have been an inside job. A Canadian news program conducted a review of the events of 9/11 to see if it had been caused deliberately by others designated as insiders rather than the hijackers. Structural engineers and architects conducted a study on the structure of the Twin Towers and provided a summary which went against what was reported by the U.S. government.

Additionally, the "pit" remaining where the Twin Towers once stood showed the heat generated in the rubble was between 500 and 700 degrees hotter than the temperature at which JetA1 fuel burns. How do we explain those high temperatures that remained within the "pit" several weeks after the attacks?

The thermal images taken by infra-red cameras revealed there was too much heat for the firefighters to clear away the rubble. Traces of a material called thermite were found in the rubble. Thermite burns at an exceedingly high temperature that melts steel. The presence of thermite traces has led to speculation that an incendiary device had been used to destroy the steel support structures of the buildings. Such speculation was based upon the assumption that deliberate acts had been taken independent of the crashes of the jet airliners to destroy the Twin Towers of the world Trade Center.

Moving on from the Twin Towers, we look at World Trade Center Building 7 which was a smaller 47 floor building some 300 feet away from the Twin Towers. Building 7 housed the IRS Regional Center, the US Secret Service, and an undisclosed CIA activity. Mayor Giuliani's Office of Emergency Management and its emergency command center were housed on the 23rd floor. The 23rd floor had recently been renovated. The upgrade included bullet and bomb resistant windows designed to withstand 200 MPH winds. The renovations were made in response to the 1993 bombing of the Towers by Omar Abdel-Rahman, an al Qaeda operative known as the blind Sheik.

On the day of the attack, Mayor Giuliani and his staff had set up their offices in a different headquarters. In an interview he said," I went down to the scene and we set up headquarters at 75 Barclay Street," abandoning the special bunker designed precisely for such an event. He told Peter Jennings of ABC news a different account. (See "Giuliani's statement) The comments made to Jennings agreed in part with the account Mayor Giuliani gave to the 9/11 Commission, but he did not tell the Commission about being "told that the World Trade Center was going to collapse" before it had collapsed.

Similar observations were reported by a BBC News reporter, Jane Stanley. She spoke about Building 7 collapsing half an hour before it happened. In video footage on YouTube Building 7 can still be seen in the background behind her as she is reporting the collapse of the Building. When questioned later a BBC spokesperson said, "If we reported the building had collapsed before it had done so, it would have been an error - no more than that."

A survey conducted by YouGov on behalf of "Architects & Engineers for 9/11 Truth" revealed a number of discrepancies in the government report on the cause of the building's collapse. They concluded after viewing videos of the collapse of Building 7 that it was not possible for Building 7 to have collapsed because of a fire, as reported.

Researchers at the University of Alaska Fairbanks came to similar conclusions that are documented in their report following a four-year computer modeling study of the tower's collapse. Their report confirmed that "Building 7 did not come down from the fires seen in the news footage shot on 911."

The government's official position in their final report on Building 7 by the National Institute for Standards and Technology (NIST) concluded that it was the fires that caused this building to collapse. The NIST report goes against the findings of the independent report created by the AE911 Truth Organization, who could not re-create the building collapse from the fires seen in the videos. Moreover, the University of Alaska Fairbanks team concluded that the findings in the government report concerning the collapse of World Trade Center Building 7 were incorrect.

Rebuttal of the Allegations

The assumption that the World Trade Center was destroyed by the impact and the fires started by the highjacked airliners was challenged by some, who claimed the Twin Towers were destroyed by an inside job. They believe unidentified rogue government actors or agencies at the state, local or federal level planted explosive or incendiary devices that brought down the Twin Towers in coordination with Arab suicide bombers flying hijacked airliners into the buildings. All of which took place on 9/11.

The allegations that US insiders destroyed the World Trade Center presumes the existence of a command-and-control cell capable of planning and directing such a complex operation. It seems unlikely that any US inside group could orchestrate the activities of Arab hijackers and US workers planting bombs to be detonated simultaneously with the aircraft crashes into the buildings. The recruiting of the Arab suicide bombers would be virtually impossible for US insiders. The US insiders would have to send the suicide bombers to the US, get them trained up as aviators in the US, while supporting them during their attendance at aviation training. (We know from their message traffic that the Arab recruiting and preparations were financed and directed by al Qaeda, not a US insider group, which contradicts the insider conspiracy theory.)

It is a conspiracy theory of massive proportions. It is difficult to imagine the challenge posed by the synchronization of the training of Arab terrorists, their hijackings of airliners, and their subsequent crashes into the World Trade Center. This activity would have to be coordinated with the US incendiary bomb makers, and laborers installing the explosives under the direction of an insider management team, that has never been identified. And then the inside group had to make it all come together on 9/11.

Rigging large buildings for destruction with demolitions and incendiary devices capable of destroying buildings the size of the World Trade Center is an enormous task. Simply planting the number of explosives and incendiary devices needed to bring down such massive structures would require an extensive workforce trained as demolition engineers months to complete. How could rigging huge buildings for demolition have been possible without discovery by the occupants of the buildings? Keeping the operation secret for months in advance would have been impossible. Someone would have leaked the workings of the conspiracy.

The details of this conspiracy theory of betrayal by insiders are worthy of examination, but they should be recognized for what they are. They are the product of speculation by academicians who have concluded that Muslims were not to blame. Rather, American insiders did the treasonous deeds that resulted in the collapse of the World Trade Center. The theory sounds like the work of people without practical experience in the US workforce.

American workers do not carry out attacks on America in compliance with orders that would have constituted treason. The visionaries assuming an inside group could pull this off do not know American workers. Could socialist academicians have motives that would absolve Moslems of responsibility for the deadly attacks, while accusing American workers of the treasonous deeds? Yes. We call it sedition and it takes place every day in the American academic community.

Although we remain agnostic regarding the events that transpired, the insider conspiracy explanation seems unlikely. A more likely scenario is that members of the Saudi Royal Family concocted the conspiracy theory to deflect criticism of the Saudi Royal family for the destruction of the Twin Towers of the World Trade Center.

They paid "experts" to conduct studies absolving the Saudi nationals for responsible for deeds that are irrefutable. The most probable explanation is that the studies implicating US insiders for the destruction of the Twin Towers were bought and paid for by the Saudi Royal Family.

Why did Mayor Giuliani occupy facilities other than the emergency operations center in Building 7 that had been built to handle such an emergency? The Mayor learned of the aircraft that had crashed into the Twin Towers shortly after the disaster occurred. As he and the members of the emergency response team approached the scene of the burning Twin Towers, it would have been too dangerous to proceed into Building 7 located 300 feet away from the Twin Towers. Moreover, the streets would have been closed by emergency response vehicles and falling debris from the burning buildings.by the time the Mayor arrived on the scene.

The WMD of Saddam Hussein

Following the 9/11 attack on the World Trade Center, President George W. Bush branded three countries, North Korea, Iran and Iraq, as rogue states saying they harbored, financed, and aided terrorists. Based on US intelligence holdings President Bush insisted that Saddam Hussein was hiding an active weapons cache of Weapons of Mass Destruction (WMD) in defiance of the United Nations ban of all chemical weapons.

The Arab terrorist community in Iraq, Iran, and Afghanistan had been resisting US efforts to bring to justice those responsible for the 9/11 attacks. On 11 February 2003 one month before the US attacked Iraq bin-Laden announced on Al-Jazeera Television that cooperation with socialists in the fight against the crusaders (US, UK) was permitted. He called on Muslims to fight in the streets against the Americans. Meanwhile, Iraq repeatedly refused the UN inspectors entry into Iraq. All attempts by the UN Security Council to enter Iraq to see for themselves were met with Saddam's repeated refusals to comply. This led to United Nations Security Council Resolution 1441 on 8 November 2002, offering Iraq a final opportunity to comply with its Resolution. Saddam's refusal to comply led to the Security Council holding Iraq in Material Breach of Iraq's disarmament obligations.

Senior American leaders were determined to take advantage of the UN Security Council decision finding Iraq in non-compliance. President Bush followed up by invading Iraq to punish Saddam Hussein for war crimes against the Kurds and to destroy his stockpile of Weapons of Mass Destruction (WMD) that were reported to be hidden in Iraq.

President Bush's intervention in Iraq involved US military forces in an invasion that led to the destruction of the Republican Guard and the demise of Saddam Hussein. The invasion, of Iraq quickly turned into a People's War as Saddam's Republican Guard were no match for the US invaders. The Iraqi forces went to ground fighting as terrorists. American troops repeatedly encountered chemical weapons in Iraq. On six occasions American troops were wounded by, chemical weapons. American troops reported that they found roughly 5,000 chemical warheads, shells, or aviation bombs in Iraq.

The WMD in Iraq were provided by the Soviet Union as military aid. The terms of the military assistance are unknown, but given the oil wealth of the Iraqi regime, it is safe to assume they were paid for by Saddam Hussein. The Soviet military assistance program was designed to thwart US military presence in the region. Consequently, we conclude that Soviet intervention had been responsible for the Red Flag concerning WMD in Iraq.

The liberal American news media were generally opposed to the Republican President and his national policy. The press missed no opportunity to oppose the President. Their hostility led to a policy of denial of US progress in the search for the WMD of Saddam Hussein. Despite the discovery of large chemical weapon stockpiles in Iraq the liberal media concluded the US discoveries of the chemical weapons did not constitute the WMD prohibited by the UN, nor justify the US invasion of Iraq.

Conclusions

The Red Flags we have addressed have been interpreted as American failures by the liberal media. They have never been resolved to the satisfaction of the Fourth Estate, historians, student of the art of war, or the public. Were the Americans opposed by Marxist opponents in each of the three Red Flag instances cited? We know it cannot be ruled out. In the case of the WMD in Iraq, we know the weapons were provided as foreign military assistance by the Soviet Union. They were the product of a long and bitter Cold War between the East and West that produced engagements in conflicts both covert and conventional necessitating extensive combat operations.

The terrorist groups in the Middle East were the recipients of Soviet military training and assistance. Members of the Egyptian, Syrian and Iraqi military received military training provided by the Soviet Union. The Soviet training increased the threats to US national interests. It also contributed to the rise in terrorist activity throughout the Middle East.

The demise of the Soviet Union in 1991 suggests a measure of success was enjoyed by the West, but the dramatic gains by the People's Republic of China over the last twenty-five years has more than offset any decline in the fortunes of the worldwide Socialist Movement. In retrospect we can take heart insofar as we have not experienced more Red Flag tragedies, which is remarkable given the massive expenditures by both side in the continuing contest between East and West. What are we to take from the controversy over the Kennedy assassination? The superpowers mutually agreed not to allow the tragedy to descend into WW III. The measures taken by LBJ protected the national interests of the USA, but they failed to convince skeptics.

What of the Twin Towers controversy? The evidence leads to the conclusion that the Saudi Royal Family took pragmatic measures to protect the reputation of the Kingdom and to minimize the potential liabilities by financing studies that "proved" the Saudi nationals who carried out the terrorist attacks did not bring down the Twin Towers. The effort produced controversy, but at the end of the day the effort could not disprove the irrefutable evidence of the terrorist strikes by Islamic terrorists financed by al Qaeda. Was it communist inspired? There is no evidence to suggest it was the result of a communist conspiracy.

Chapter 14:

US BATTLES WITH PEOPLE'S WAR

We live in a perilous time of change that threatens American heritage, the Constitution, and the Republic. It is the culmination of long years of change experienced during a century of confrontation between Communism and the Constitutional Republic established by the founders in 1776. In this chapter we look at lessons from the long clash between East and West over the right of the people to grow rice on their own land versus the right of the state to own all the land, as well as the means of production. It is the fundamental struggle between liberty and tyranny. In previous chapters, we examined the methods used to wage the class struggle. Here we ask what we learned from decades of combatting communist revolutionaries at home and abroad?

My introduction to communist insurgency came in 1962 when President John F. Kennedy asked for volunteers to serve as advisers in Vietnam. This was the same JFK, who had challenged my generation to bear any burden in defense of freedom. Now the President was appealing for volunteers from the ranks of Seventh Army that was standing guard in Central Europe. I was a lieutenant in Seventh Army. JFK was asking me to go to war in defense of Freedom -- a far heavier burden than serving in NATO. How could I refuse? My country had paid for my education and training at West Point. I offered my service as a volunteer and so began my participation in the long quest for understanding Peoples War that became the great challenge of my generation.

In Vietnam we discovered to our dismay that the enemy owned the allegiance of American intellectuals. They were the establishment elite that included journalists, college professors, Hollywood celebrities and the anchormen and women on the evening television news. Whereas the domestic enemy we faced were graduates of the most exclusive schools and colleges in the country, the soldiers serving in uniform reflected the common people (HRC's deplorables), who loved the USA and bravely sacrificed in the line of duty. The American people were made up of middle-class citizens, as well as rural country folk. They were farmers, merchants, steel workers, coal miners and construction workers, who proudly served in uniform in defense of freedom.

There was a noticeable distance between the soldiers serving in uniform and the intellectual elite of the country. The intellectuals had few if any loyalties to the flag. Their loyalties were to progressive teachings that considered socialism to be more just than the American free enterprise system. There was a vast difference between the fidelity of the soldier and the infidelity of the intellectual. That distance was immeasurably increased when college students were granted deferments from the draft. It was an unfortunate decision that transformed colleges into bastions of opposition to the war and sanctuaries for draft dodgers, pacifists, and student radicals. Many graduates of that generation of anti-war activists went on to become college professors who proceeded to pass on their socialist beliefs to the next generation.

The draft deferments were contingent upon maintaining passing grades, which placed pressure on faculty and students alike. Faculty members were too conflicted to flunk students knowing they could be drafted and soon serving in combat. The solution arrived at by faculty members was to inflate grades so that all students received passing grades. It was a solution that compromised standards of excellence allowing substandard work to become the norm. Inflation of college grades had the unintended consequence of diminishing the value of a college education making college diplomas suspect.

Those who opposed America's role as defender of the South Vietnamese people from North Vietnamese aggression included college professors, journalists, Hollywood stars, clergy, and student radicals. They justified their opposition to the war by attacking the cause for which we fought. They turned their anger on the men and women serving in uniform on the Home Front. With the benefit of hindsight, we recognized the unity of effort between enemy infantry assaults in distant jungle combat and domestic opponents of the war, who burned the flag and trashed the reputations of American servicemen and women. Vietnamese communist troops and American student radicals were united in their hatred for America and the free enterprise system.

Why the parallels between events halfway round the world? The war in Vietnam was part of the larger Sino-Soviet strategy to liberate the Third World from ties to the West and the free enterprise system. It was part of the global Soviet strategy to defeat American led containment of communism. Mao Zedong's strategy was to wage asymmetrical warfare using communist insurgencies that the West was ill equipped to resist. Mao mobilized peasant armies to wage People's War against the armed forces of the Western Democracies that held communist conquest of Asia in check by their stand in South Korea, Japan, Taiwan, Malaysia, South Vietnam, and the Philippines.

Tackling People's Wars

The fight against People's Wars was long and bloody. Initially, it was exceedingly difficult going for America and its allies. The enemy was using a pattern of warfare perfected in rural China during the decades-long Chinese Communist Civil Wars and the United Front war against Japanese Imperialism. After many clashes between the Americans and the National Liberation Front, the CIA broke the code. The American intelligence learned to avoid the enemy on the terrain the VC and the PAVN had prepared for battle. Instead of fighting the enemy on his ground, the Vietnamese people and the Saigon regime took the war to the enemy by striking the communist power base.

The battle was directed by the CIA, who were remarkably effective once the Americans learned how the enemy fought. Instead of attacking battle position occupied by dug in infantry, the CIA attacked the NLF rear area and its vulnerable recruiters, party cadre and their clandestine cell structure. The attacks were conducted by the Vietnamese people, who wanted no part of People's War.

The People of South Vietnam knew all about People's War. They had seen it at work during the war of the Vietminh to defeat French Colonialism. The Vietminh had fought with the assistance of Chinese Communist advisors from the PLA, who taught the Vietminh how to wage People's War. Mao's People's War was clandestine insurgency perfected in the wars against the KMT and Japanese Imperialism. The war was grim. It was dirty and it defeated the French, who surrendered to the Vietminh in 1954. The secrets of Mao's clandestine warfare included his recruitment techniques, his combat tactics, and his organizational structure that were all part of the Maoist model of revolution (discussed in Chapter 6).

The Vietnamese people had gotten a nose full of the communist cadre who had taken the lives of their loved ones. The Vietminh cadre annihilated the middle class, the landowners, the merchants, and government teachers and medical staff trained by the French. Also killed were the religious believers including Roman Catholic priests and their congregations. As a result, the people had good reason to oppose the communists. The CIA solution was to arm the Vietnamese people in every village in the countryside.

The people had seen the Marxist class warfare and they wanted no part of it. Once armed and taught how to seek out the communist recruiters and cadre, the Vietnamese people destroyed Mao's People's War. They rounded up and killed the recruiters and cadre, who built the village level communist governing bodies and the guerrilla units that waged the revolutionary struggle. By 1972 the battle was over. People's War had failed. The people of South Vietnam had destroyed the Communist Party of South Vietnam, the Lao Dung Party.

The American CIA organized and directed the War against the communists using a program known as the Phoenix Program. The CIA does not get much credit for its work conducted in the shadows. Giving public recognition to the men and women of the CIA who organized and directed the fight would be suicidal. The communists would assassinate them one at a time as retribution for their victory. (Hello! Wherever you are concealed in the secrecy of the shadows, take a bow men and women of the CIA. You were magnificent!)

People's War inside the USA

Mao's efforts to mobilize peasant armies to liberate Asia from American led deterrence had been focused on Vietnam as a test case of People's War. Mao strategy was linked to Soviet policy that called on the international socialist movement to support resistance against the American containment strategy. Accordingly, the Vietnam War was accompanied by a rise in Marxist rebellions in Europe featuring the Red Brigade and the Bader- Meinhof Gang. In Latin America Fidel Castro and Che Guevara attempted to launch communist insurrections, while SDS, the Black Panthers and the Weathermen spearheaded the revolution in America. The American Marxist rebellion began in the academic community and quickly spread to the liberal media, Hollywood, and main street America. It precipitated a decline in law and order across the country.

The assault on law and order was accompanied by efforts to break down traditional standards of morality in America. The German professors from the Frankfurt School who had earlier introduced critical theory studies in the American academic community, advocated free love. The free love assault on morality accompanied the feminist revolution, both of which attacked the family and discouraged traditional religious observances. They were results that did little to provoke student radicals, who were secular humanists. The free love campaign was ballyhooed by radical activists who championed the recreational use of drugs and showcased long hair and Bohemian styles of dress. They were dubbed hippies, who rejected the traditional beliefs of their parents while flaunting free love in hastily formed communal cohabitation arrangements.

The Hippie movement sparked a gold rush in the pop music industry and rock concert business. The anti-war culture resonated with innovation as gifted new artists promoted a renaissance in popular music and especially anti-war ballads. The popularity of the movement sealed the fate of any remaining hopes to win the hearts and minds of the American people in favor of the South Vietnamese cause. Rock and country music struck it rich with popular songs that made fools of the military. Encouraged by the deluge of popular support, protestors filled the streets and laid siege to the Pentagon.

The Hippies had won the day and LBJ began looking for an exit strategy from Vietnam with the help of his Pentagon generals who were left to clean up the mess left behind by Secretary of Defense Bob McNamara and his Whiz Kids. McNamara came clean on public television weeping and denouncing the war strategy he had advocated in Vietnam. He was allowed to escape and evade responsibility taking a coveted position as President of the World Bank. Poor fellow, he had been embarrassed by hostile media coverage and the popular victory of the opposing protest movement on the Home Front.

In retrospect it was ironic that despite the US defeat of Mao's celebrated People's War in Vietnam, courtesy of the CIA's Phoenix Program, American leadership found it necessary to scuttle the war effort. The administration smelled an ugly defeat in the upcoming presidential elections due to the explosion of popular resistance on the Home Front. LBJ threw in the towel telling the American People: I will not run for another term as your President.

We had lost. My generation of soldiers the Left had already branded as war criminals were now to be cast in the role of losers. All that remained was Nixon's "exit with honor" strategy behind a smoke screen of a negotiated peace settlement worked out at the Paris Peace talks by Henry Kissinger. Despite delaying tactics used by the North Vietnamese side, Kissinger prevailed with the help of B-52 Christmas bombing strikes on Hanoi and Haiphong to encourage sincerity on the part of Hanoi's negotiators.

Elsewhere the cultural war attacked all things associated with Judeo-Christian culture. The Left demonstrated their intolerance for religious beliefs by enforcement of secular demands for the separation of Church and State that sought to prohibit public displays of religious symbols and customs. Public observance of Christmas became the target of attacks by the Left, while public displays of religious worship were banished. Prayers at public events and in the classroom were banned. And crucifixes disappeared from the classrooms of the Jesuit professors at Georgetown University in Washington, DC.

Members of the academic community and Hollywood celebrities openly supported Hanoi accusing American troops of heinous war crimes. Their support of the enemy constituted sedition. In a grievous display of the decline of the rule of law in America, the Department of Justice (DOJ) and the FBI refused to prosecute even the most flagrant cases of treason by the Left. This miscarriage of justice convinced the Left that they were above the law, a travesty which continues to this day. Sadly, the problem has deteriorated since the chaotic days of the Vietnam War.

A generation after LBJ threw in the towel, the FBI and the DOJ were thoroughly politicized during the Obama administration. Under the leadership of Attorney General Erick Holder left-wing lawyers and academic radicals advocating racial insurrection were hired to staff the Department. Holder's DOJ proceeded to intimidate law enforcement officials by open support of left-wing radicals inciting mob violence. The DOJ prosecuted members of the GOP for any conduct that could be construed as criminal, while they shielded Democrats from prosecution for serious criminal conduct. This betrayal of the American tradition of liberty and justice for all signaled widespread corruption at the highest levels of the federal government. It demonstrated the American criminal justice system had been subverted for partisan political advantage.

Targets for subversion and attacks by the Left included the K-12 educational system, churches and synagogues, police and law enforcement agencies and gun rights groups that resisted efforts to restrict gun ownership. Colleges and universities caved under the weight of Marxist educators and the curtailment of First Amendment freedoms by politically correct edicts. Fortunately, not every college was captured by the Marxists. The Military Academy at West Point continued to graduate platoon leaders faithful to the USA, but the Military Academy faculty was under relentless pressure as intellectuals worked overtime to undermine faith in God and country. American values were attacked from all sides by liberal establishment elites.

The Fourth Estate

The free press that once stood guard over free speech and democracy in America vanished overnight. The liberal media joined the ranks of the progressives rejecting free enterprise and the Constitution. Instead of safeguarding freedom, they used heavy handed censorship to silence critics of the Left, while they actively supported liberals propagating the socialist line. Liberal journalists made up of socialists and fellow travelers now ruled the roost, where they savaged Americans and their history. While not every democrat of the period was a radical, every radical of the period was a democrat.

In Chapter 2 we documented gaslighting by the fourth estate in Vietnam. The gaslighting concealed Hanoi's leadership in directing the war in Vietnam and covered up the war crimes committed by North Vietnamese soldiers in their conquest of South Vietnam. These transgressions by journalists against their responsibility for fair and balanced treatment of the news demonstrated the liberal media had adopted the socialist doctrine of the enemy soldiers we faced on the field of battle. The Fourth Estate's lack of fidelity to America still prevails today and is unconstitutional, a violation of freedom of the press and a fundamental flaw in our Republic. This tragic betrayal of America by the men and women of the Fourth Estate has rendered the Republic a housed divided that cannot long endure as Abraham Lincoln famously observed of the Union on the eve of the Civil War.

One of the unpleasant realities of the War in Vietnam was covered-up by the media. The brutal character of the peasant soldiers of North Vietnam and their massive atrocities were concealed by journalists covering the War. The peasant soldiers of the People's Army of Vietnam (PAVN) savagely murdered thousands of innocent villagers as they carried out Lenin's vision of a classless society. We are what we do is a fundamental truth of the human condition. Those who kill are killers. Those who murder thousands of innocent villagers because they are Roman Catholic, or Buddhists, or supporters of the Saigon regime are savage murderers.

Communist soldiers, who act as executioners in annihilating entire social classes are fundamentally different from American soldiers, who defend the constitution. For example, the soldiers of Communist China, who routinely commit crimes against humanity to preserve communist rule are brutal thugs. Conversely, the soldiers of liberal societies who defend freedom reflect the values of their liberal societies. Since we are what we do, our personalities and character mirror our deeds. Thus, communist soldiers, who murder in the name of the state, are predictably brutal thugs. These gruesome traits of the invading North Vietnamese soldiers were covered-up by journalists covering the War from Saigon, who did a disservice to their readers by concealing a glaring reality.

The Preservation of the American Heritage

In the cultural war of the Left against all things celebrating American Heritage, the Left trashed all testimonials to national heritage. The customs, symbols, and dignity of the past were viciously attacked. Monuments celebrating war heroes came under attack as the left ruthlessly smeared all things reflecting American pride. Antifa and Black Lives Matter carried out a scorched earth strategy to discredit American heritage. Our heroes were mocked. Their statues were defaced and torn down.

Athletes were pressured to mock the American Flag by taking a knee in protest when the national anthem was played. Naïve athletes played along with the demands of their radical peers by raising their clenched fists and kneeling to show disrespect for the American Flag and the Republic for which it stands. It was a clear message to impressionable youngsters that America was evil. It was a public declaration of their rejection of American citizenship.

By kneeling during the playing of the anthem protesters are saying they reject the flag, the Republic and American citizenship. This hostile act toward the USA makes the perpetrators aliens. Moreover, their hostility towards the Flag demonstrates they are adversaries who are ineligible to participate in public events or to remain in the country. Had they tried this disrespect in Woodrow Wilson's day they would have ended up in jail.

Caring for the Survivors

We have previously observed that communist soldiers who commit crimes against humanity are turned into brutal thugs. We also have observed that soldiers of liberal societies who defend freedom are fundamentally different from soldiers of communist dictatorships, who commit crimes against humanity.

The soldiers of liberal societies defend the constitution. In so doing their character is preserved from the dehumanizing influence of massive human slaughter incident to building a Marxist society. Nevertheless, American soldier do fight in close combat to defend freedom. The infantry and the cavalry close with and destroy the enemy in close combat. All combat to include defending freedom is a brutalizing experience that robs soldiers of their innocence. It hardens character. In some cases the experience leaves emotional scares that can become permanent. Some of these warriors experience PTSD that we examined in Chapter 12.

Enemy propaganda that is used to attack combat effectiveness is destructive to troop morale. The charges by Hanoi that American soldiers were war criminals were false. It was Hanoi's troops who were required to carry out mass murder in accordance with Hanoi's policy. These atrocities were war crimes. Even though Hanoi's allegations that Americans soldiers were war criminals were untrue, American troop morale was hurt by the charges. The allegations that we were war criminals were especially demoralizing for the wounded, who had made great sacrifices in combat. Studies funded by the VA revealed that the death rate from all causes for wounded soldiers suffering from PTSD was twice that of soldiers without PTSD.

Militant protesters on the Home Front who portrayed American soldiers as war criminals (e.g., Jane Fonda and John Kerry) served to destroy public confidence in American policy, to increase desertion rates, and to increase the death rate from wounds sustained in combat. These unfortunate outcomes were preventable. Had the DOJ been enforcing the law both Fonda and Kerry would have been behind bars for acts of treason. Had the DOJ done their duty, Fonda's and Kerry's criminal behavior would have posed no threat to society or soldiers vulnerable to the harmful effects of enemy propaganda. Regrettably, the failure of the DOJ had serious adverse consequences for American soldiers. Dereliction of duty has serious consequences for society that we ignore at our peril.

The Final Outcome

It was on the Home Front that the decisive battles of the Vietnam War were fought. The Left won the public support needed to take control of Congress where they outlawed American support for South Vietnam resulting in unilateral capitulation by the American side.

America's confrontation with People's War ended in a draw. While America capitulated after suffering defeat on the Home Front, People's War was defeated by the US on the battlefield in South Vietnam. Hanoi was forced to wage a conventional campaign to conquer South Vietnam. They fought no differently than did the conventual armies of the West. We conclude that whereas America defeated People's War in Asia, People's War defeated America on the Home Front.

After sustaining multiple defeats on the Home Front over the last two generations, the constitutional order is in danger. Following the 2020 election the Democrats took control of the Executive Branch. They took control of both houses of Congress. Moreover, the Democrats appear to have won control of the Supreme Court that is behaving like a Democrat-controlled Court. Given the socialist agenda of the Left, the Constitution is in grave danger. Whether the Republic can survive the next four years remains to be seen. We will examine the crisis facing America in the next Chapter.

Chapter 15:

THE LOST SOVEREIGNTY OF THE PEOPLE

American democracy and the constitutional order have been put to the test by a calculated coup that stole the 2020 presidential election. The coup abandoned time-honored American tradition, ignored the Constitution, and eviscerated the rule of law. In this Chapter we will assess the situation confronting America. We will look at where we are today and how we got to where we are. And finally, we will define the task that lies before us. The first requirement is to look at the hard truth. What happened and why?

When the Democratic Party cannot win honestly, they lie, cheat, and steal, which reflects Saul Alinsky's doctrine. That's exactly what Saul told them to do. They are playing according to Saul. They could not win the 2020 election honestly. They won it by changing the rules that govern elections using executive orders and court orders that were unconstitutional. The constitution says only the state legislature can make the rules that govern elections. They won it by stuffing ballot boxes with bogus ballots for Joe Biden, which was illegal. They got away with it because the liberal journalists only told one side of the story and the courts refused to hear the other side of the story. Everybody who counted was pulling for Joe and they were all Democrats.

When the Democrats cannot win the policy debate, they kill the message, if not the messenger and the horse he rode in on. The Democrats turned their backs on a policy debate in 2020 because the facts did not support their man. Instead, they made the campaign about the personality of the President. They made their presidential campaign about character assassination. Why? Because Trump had all the answers the people wanted to hear. His solutions fixed the real problems confronting middle class Americans. So the Democrats worked overtime to kill Trump's reputation and with it his future as a GOP candidate for office.

President Trump's articulation of the issues was riveting. He dominated the policy debates. He could talk for two hours with no teleprompter and no notes. They had no chance of winning an honest debate. So, showing their concern for public safety, they canceled the last debate as a virus Pandemic precaution. Instead, they waged a vicious character assassination campaign to destroy the man who fixed the problems. They impeached the former President accusing him of the sin they had been committing across the country all summer – insurrection.

The 2020 presidential election was stolen in a coup that saw the rise to power of socialist demagogues. The crisis had been brewing for years. Over the last generation, Americans saw their country steadily decline. The precipitous decline began when the GOP lost the 1992 presidential campaign. The archconservative H. Ross Perot ran against George H. W. Bush on a third-party ticket handing the White House over to the Democrats. It was an unforced error that derailed a sure victory by the winner of the Gulf War, President George H. W. Bush, who had enjoyed a substantial lead over his democratic opponent going into the election.

Gotterdammerung

Following World War II, the US economy encountered the resurgent power of rebuilt European economies as well as the power of a thriving Japanese economy, which resulted in a gradual economic retraction in America. The gradual US economic decline became serious during Bill Clinton's two terms in office. The reduction of the American manufacturing base, the theft of intellectual property, and the dumping of cheap foreign products on the market resulted in the loss of heavy industry and manufacturing jobs, an increase in the trade deficit and a decline in the earnings of the middle class. The US steel industry gradually shut down and American jobs were exported to China. Bill

Clinton contributed to the economic decline by bad decisions that obligated the administration in ways unseen in previous administrations.

Following Clinton's inauguration, Bill and Hillary occupied the White House with their hippie friends. Bill and Hillary had invited friends from Arkansas and college days to fill hundreds of positions on the White House staff. Some arrived at the White House on motorcycles wearing blue jeans and t-shirts. The Secret Service was appalled by the Hippies, many of whom were unqualified to hold a security clearance that was required to work in the White House.

The FBI was responsible for conducting background investigations required before staff members were granted a security clearance. The FBI requested the newcomers fill out background documentation and participate in interviews to commence the clearance process. The new staff were granted temporary passes to allow them to pass through White House security until security clearances were granted and permanent passes could be issued.

Having spent their wayward youths doing drugs and hanging out with radical agitators many of the new staff had established records they had no intention of sharing with the FBI. They simply refused to cooperate with the FBI by filling out the security questionnaires and participating in the interviews with the FBI agents. By their refusal to cooperate with the FBI agents a stand-off was created that threated to bring the FBI clearance process to a halt.

The Clintons solved the problem by establishing new White House operating procedures that allowed the staff to operate pretty much as they had while Bill was Governor of Arkansas. They redesigned the temporary security passes to resemble permanent passes, while making no effort to require the new staff to cooperate with the FBI to obtain security clearances. The White House Counsel issued instructions that did not permit the FBI to share the results of background checks with the Secret Service. In so doing the Clinton White House established new operating procedures that allowed their new staff members to work in the White House and to handle classified information without a security clearance. It was unprecedented doing away with security procedures that had been in place since Eisenhower was President.[36]

The predicament was in keeping with the Clintons' history that showed a tendency for contrarian Bohemian conduct as ardent followers of Saul Alinsky. Be that as it may, the new occupants of the White House from Arkansas were looking for new opportunities. The Clintons rented out the Lincoln bedroom in the White House to tourists, sold government property for personal gain, and they opened the doors to Communist China's unethical operations in America in return for their financial support of Bill's presidential campaign.

The agenda of the Clintons was consistent with the Alinsky doctrine that directs followers to attack the United

---

[36] Gary Aldrich, Unlimited Access, (Regnery Publishing, Washington, 1996), pages 52-65.

States from within. From his earliest days in office, President Clinton set out to even the playing field by reducing the super-power advantages of the US in favor of Clinton's financial backers in Communist China. President Clinton reduced the size of the US armed forces by 40 %. He disregarded the foreign policy of his predecessors in the oval office by pursuit of inconsequential foreign policy objectives thereby wasting American lives and treasure for purposes that did not enhance American interests. He removed or reduced classification safeguards that protected top-secret information including US nuclear deterrence capabilities. In so doing Clinton collaborated with America's enemies by facilitating the compromise of the design of American nuclear weapons systems. [37]

Clinton's declassification initiative placed top secret information at risk by exposing defense programs to enemy espionage. A Chinese spy by the name of Wen Ho Lee, an American citizen employed by the Los Alamos Nuclear Laboratory, downloaded top-secret files of the Laboratory onto his personal computer. The personal computer served as a dead drop that was used to pass the most highly classified US technical secrets to the PRC. Clinton's declassification efforts coupled with the dead drop provided by Wen Ho Lee are credited with providing the

---

[37] David Horowitz, *Black Book of the American Left Volume VII: The Left in Power, Clinton to Obama* (Second Thought Books; Los Angeles, 2015) pages 85 to 94.

PLA with advanced technology equivalent to twenty years' worth of research and development. [38]

The Clintons established The Clinton Foundation, a faux charity, to manage the illicit cash flow stemming from the sale of US property. Sale of US assets included the sale of top secret classified information to the PRC, the sale of Stinger missiles to al-Qaeda, the sale of Uranium to Russia, and the sale of access to senior US officials to foreign leaders. The email scandal of Hillary Clinton addressed the unlawful destruction of an estimated 30,000 messages under subpoena by Congress containing evidence corroborating the sale of US property and access to US officials by the Clintons.

World affairs were in a state of flux at the time Bill Clinton took office. With the collapse of the Soviet Union in 1991, the US enjoyed unrivaled supremacy as the lone surviving superpower. US deterrence responsibilities were relaxed, which ushered in a period of peace unseen since Herbert Hoover was president. Regrettably, Clinton missed an unrivaled opportunity to advance US national interests by taking a foreign affairs holiday and abandoning a strong national defense. Despite a poor showing in statecraft, Clinton managed to demonstrate America's new role in foreign affairs that can be described as aberrant. Instead of serving American national interests, Clinton's foreign policy was fashioned to allow Bill to be seen as an actor on the world stage.

---

[38] Dan Stober and Ian Hoffman, A *Convenient Spy*: *Wen Ho Lee and the Politics of Nuclear Espionage*, *(Simon and Shuster; New York, 2001).*

Sadly, Bill Clinton chose to exercise his presidential authority by intervening in affairs in which the US had no national interests. He badly botched a US intervention in Somalia, a failed state that functioned as a base for international pirates and drug traffickers. The intervention employed inadequate military forces that resulted in a massacre of Army rangers that became known as Black Hawk Down. Requests for reinforcements by the military commander in Somalia had been denied by White House staffers.

The Somalian intervention was followed by an intervention in a Balkans conflict between Muslims and Christians that had been underway since the capture of Constantinople by the Ottoman Turks in the Fifteenth Century. Clinton sided with the Muslims against the Christians; a move that mirrored his domestic policy that favored Muslims over Christians. In the end, the US expended American blood and treasure for causes that did nothing to advance US national interests.

Clinton's lack of experience in statecraft invited aggressive challenges by terrorists, rogue nations, and petty dictators. In a dramatic escalation of terrorist activity, the World Trade Center was bombed and three American embassies plus the American Military Mission Headquarters in Riyadh were destroyed by Al Qaeda terrorists. The US responses were ineffective symbolic gestures. Bill fired some missiles into the desert and set a pharmaceutical factory on fire, which accomplished nothing other than to put some hapless laborers out of work. If that were not enough bad news for the legacy of the forty-second President of the United States, during Clinton's watch US trade policy allowed Globalists to further Chinese efforts to dismantle the US manufacturing sector thereby exporting more American jobs to Third World nations.

Prior to leaving office Bill Clinton was exposed as a sexual molester. He was revealed as a sexual predator with a history of sexually abusing subordinates that resulted in his impeachment. (In a rough comparison, one could say that Bill Clinton had done for the US what Lenin had done for Russian society, i.e., he destroyed much of the middle class.)

Clinton was followed in the White House by George W. Bush, who brought a measure of stability and a return to serving the national interests to government. Military readiness again became a priority. Regrettably, Americans saw the national debt dramatically increase and homeland security shattered following the 9/11 terrorist attacks. Saudi Nationals practicing what President Bush called a religion of peace carried out the attacks. US Representative Ilhan Omar later clarified events cryptically saying that *"Some people did something."* [39]

---

[39] US Representative to Congress Ilhan Omar from the 5th District of Minnesota used these words to describe the World Trade Center attack by Arab terrorists from Saudi Arabia on 9/11. Her words were intended to deflect responsibility for the attacks from her fellow Muslims.

Under the Bush administration the American economy continued to decline. George Bush was a globalist visionary like his father. Consequently, no action was taken to halt the theft of the US manufacturing base in America's heartland. The trade imbalance with Communist China increased as the Chinese continued to steal intellectual property and maintained their unfair trade practices. Thus, the long-term decline of job growth and wages continued during the Bush administration.

In foreign affairs President Bush suffered the consequences of Clinton's foreign affairs holiday that resulted in the 9/11 disaster, which demolished the World Trade Center. Bush reacted to the disaster by attacking the Taliban in Afghanistan that had provided sanctuary and training to Islamic terrorists. The Taliban was driven from power and a war of attrition was begun in Afghanistan that would last for the next twenty years. The Americans were reenforced by a NATO presence that forced al Qaeda and the Taliban to seek refuge in Pakistan and mountain sanctuaries.

An indigenous government was formed that attempted to bring secular government and democracy to the people of Afghanistan. How long that government can survive following the NATO withdrawal remains to be seen. If the precedents established by the ancient Greeks, the British, and the Soviet occupations of Afghanistan are any indication of future events, the prospects for survival of the secular Afghani government are less than auspicious.

President Bush followed up his nation building in Afghanistan by invading Iraq to punish Saddam Hussein for war crimes against the Kurds and to destroy the Iraqi stockpile of weapons of mass destruction (WMD). The stockpile of banned Iraqi chemical weapons justified the UN approval of the US intervention that captured and destroyed approximately 5000 chemical munitions.

The Iraq invasion quickly turned into a People's War as Saddam's Republican Guard, who were no match for the US invaders, went to ground fighting as terrorists. In an effort to pacify dissidents and still internal strife, Bush armed the Muslim Shiites starting a religious war. Shiite and Sunni Muslims fought for political control of Baghdad resulting in widespread fighting and a large increase in the number of refugees. Bush's attempts to export democracy to Iraq excited the imagination but had little chance for success. Democracy challenges Sharia Law, which makes long term survival of democracy a high-risk endeavor in a Muslim country as President Erdogan's overthrow of the secular government in Turkey demonstrates.

The American interventions in Iraq and Afghanistan turned Iranian IED bomb making into a growth industry but appear to have done little to advance US national interests. The only clear winner from Bush's nation building ventures was Iran that enjoyed a windfall victory over Iraq, when their arch-rival in the region, suffered a devastating defeat at the hands of the Americans.

In 2008 Barak Hussein Obama was elected as the forty-fourth president of the United States. Upon assuming office, Obama made a world tour in which he apologized profusely for America, for being an American, and for American dominance (peace keeping). Few conservatives had any idea what Obama was talking about. Obama received the Nobel Peace Prize as a "kick in the leg" to his GOP rival, which evidently made sense in Oslo, but was incomprehensible in the USA.

On the advice of the Muslim Brotherhood, Obama revised the combat rules of engagement employed in the Middle East. He directed that weapons were to be unloaded when soldiers went into combat. Soldiers were not permitted to fire on targets unless they had been fired upon first. The new rules decreased mission effectiveness and dramatically increased casualties. Meanwhile, Obama directed the military to report that combat operations were successful in destroying al Qaeda, which was not true. Intelligence analysts continued to submit reports indicating al Qaeda was gaining in strength. It was information the President did not want to hear, which infuriated Obama.

It was a bad time to be a Pentagon briefing officer for the president. The resistance to unethical pressure on the intelligence community preserved the integrity of the intelligence collection effort, while it served to make Lieutenant General Mike Flynn an enemy of the President.

Obama directed domestic terrorist attacks be called "workplace violence" and that training materials containing information critical of Islamic terrorists be removed from classrooms. In another move that showed his support for Islamic terrorists, Obama released most of the terrorist prisoners incarcerated in Guantanamo Bay, many of whom returned to fight in the ranks of al Qaeda and other terrorist groups. Meanwhile, the President slashed the defense budget, reduced the US nuclear weapons inventory, and unilaterally disarmed the USA. Based on his actions, it was hard to escape the impression that the Commander-in-Chief was abandoning the soldiers who fought under his command.

Another explanation for the president's behavior was the possibility that the President was not a natural born American citizen. At times President Obama's actions appeared to be those of a Third World nationalist getting even for colonialism by punishing the West. It was behavior that mystified Americans. However, the President's behavior made sense if you were born in East Africa as a citizen of a former British colony. The Democrats vehemently denied reports Obama had been born in Nairobi, while the media decried efforts by birthers to deny a "native son" his birthrights.

In a stunning display of disloyalty, President Obama ordered the American military to pull out of Iraq, thereby dismantling efforts of the Bush administration to establish Iraq as an American partner in the region. Obama's actions rendered the sacrifices of American soldiers meaningless. All the blood and treasure NATO had invested in pacification of Iraq had been wasted. The unilateral US capitulation allowed the Iranians to fill the power vacuum left by the hasty US departure, thereby acquiring a windfall of military hardware left behind by the Americans.

Foreign policy experts were baffled when Obama made a treaty with Iran that permitted the Mullahs to acquire nuclear weapons. Ironically Obama sweetened the deal by giving the Mullahs $1.7 billion in cash. (The lead negotiator on the US side was John Kerry, the former member of the Vietnam Veterans Against the War, who had briefed the Senate Foreign Affairs Subcommittee on American war crimes.)

Elsewhere, Obama appeared to be acting like a true statesman by drawing a red line in Syria to end the use of chemical weapons against civilians. The appearance of American resolve quickly dissolved when Obama failed to take any action when the red line was ignored. Obama increased the impact of the PR fiasco in Syria by inviting the Russians to take control of the situation, which surrendered America's sphere of influence in the region to the Russians.

Obama intervened in Egyptian politics by assisting the Muslim Brotherhood in their quest for political power. His intervention sparked the killing of Coptic Christians and alienated the Egyptian officer corps, resulting in a short tenure for the regime of the Muslim Brotherhood. In neighboring Libya, President Obama sanctioned Secretary of State Hillary Clinton's intervention to bring about regime change triggering a war that severely hurt American and European interests.

Overall, Obama's interventions in the region had been a disaster. By pulling the plug in Iraq, failing to intervene in Syria, starting a war in Libya, handing Syria to the Russians, and allowing the Iranians to acquire WMD he had destabilized the region. Obama's interventions turned the region into a bloodbath with fighting in Afghanistan, Iraq, Lebanon, Syria, Yemen, Libya, and with the Kurds of the region. The chaos would cause a tsunami of refugees that soon inundated Turkey, Greece, and central Europe.

Elsewhere the Obama administration sold arms to Muslim terrorists which made no sense unless it was theft of government property for personal gain. A stinger missile fired at an American helicopter in Afghanistan was recovered as a dud. The serial number of the missile identified it as an American missile that had been sold to terrorists by Hillary Clinton. To cover-up the illicit weapons deal, the American Ambassador to Libya was sent to Benghazi to negotiate a deal with al Quade to recover the missiles. The Ambassador was killed by the terrorists along with four other Americans in a well-executed terrorist attack.

A clumsy cover up of the illicit arms smuggling operation revealed Obama officials in a particularly bad light lying to the public on five different Sunday morning television shows. The cover story was that the Ambassador had died because of a spontaneous demonstration. The cover story fell apart as soon as the survivors of the Benghazi incident had an opportunity to tell their story, which revealed the full extent of the corruption of the Obama administration.

At home Obama advanced the cause of socialism by signing legislation approving universal health care, which was a disaster that was mismanaged and dysfunctional creating more problems than it solved. Elsewhere on the domestic front, Obama directed the Little Sisters of the Poor to distribute birth control pills, a cynical move that no doubt prompted hilarious laughter behind closed doors.

Having unilaterally disarmed America by defunding the Pentagon, Obama approved the introduction of women into the combat branches of the military services. He added to the demoralization he had created in the ranks by directing the Pentagon to allow the entry of transgender individuals into the military. Obama's actions reduced combat readiness and were the equivalent of assigning high school dropouts as analysts in the Office of Management and Budget (OMB).

Obama authorized massive spending programs to fund development of green energy that employed crony capitalism that funneled billions of dollars to campaign donors who became multi-millionaires overnight. In a less well-known scheme Obama used federal hiring as payment for personal favors creating public servants that used public office (e.g., IRS, DOJ, FBI) to advance Democratic Party interests. In a monumental misuse of federal agencies, Obama officials spied on the Trump Campaign seeking dirt to hurt the rival presidential candidate.

The Obama scandals amounted to unprecedented corruption. If Obama's purpose in office was to ruin capitalists and so-called neo-colonial nations, his malicious endeavors were highly successful. Saul Alinsky would have been proud of him. (To fully appreciate the scale of the disaster, one could equate the impact of Obama's destructive policies upon the USA and the Middle East with the devastation Adolph Hitler inflicted on Central Europe. American and Middle Eastern cities lay in ruins like the destruction of the cities of the Third Reich following WW II.)

A Republic in Name Only

The level of corruption in the Executive branch during Obama's time in office had been unprecedented. Regrettably, the corruption on Capitol Hill was equally serious. Instead of honoring their oath of office, many Congressional representatives ditched their responsibilities to the people, while accepting bribes in return for legislation that advanced commercial interests both at home and abroad. The US Congress sold American jobs, opened borders to illegal trafficking and provided commercial advantages to foreign interests in return for lavish cash payments to the Congressmen. The representatives of the people had acted as thieves and tyrants.

The neglect of their responsibilities by Congressional representatives denied the people their voice in government. The people, who are sovereign in America, were told to go away and shut up by Speaker of the House John Boehner. The Speaker had bigger fish to fry. He was busy passing important legislation paid for with bribes from big donors making it possible for the globalist coalition of big business to plunder middle America. In the process, the people were disenfranchised by the loss of their voices in the direction of Congress. The result was the USA no longer had a functioning representative form of government.

The people were no longer sovereign in America as established by the Constitution. The legislative branch of government was illegally exercising political power without the consent of the governed. The American constitutional Republic had been transformed into a despotic form of government by usurpation of the authority that had been granted to the people by the founders. Speaker Boehner was guilty of high crimes against the Constitution of the United States of America. Impeachment was too good a fate for the crook, but it never happened because the Congress had bought into taking cash under the table in return for legislative favors.

The chief executive was equally unresponsive to the voices of the people. Government by, for and of the people was defunct. It was a constitutional crisis that fundamentally altered the framework of the Republic established by the founders. It was time for change that appeared in the form of a grass roots rebellion that saw the electorate rise and demand reforms from a Congress that no longer cared what the people thought.

Deliverance

In the midst of this national crisis a hero emerged, who promised that if elected he would restore the sovereignty of the people. He also promised to make America great again. Donald J. Trump was a man of the people. He spoke their language. He promised to bring back jobs, to bring back fair trade, to lower taxes, to restore national borders, to end foreign wars, and to make America great again. The people elected Donald J. Trump as the forty-fifth president in a landslide.

Over the next four years, President Trump kept his promises. He built a wall and restored the borders. He lowered taxes. He restored the armed forces and reformed the Veterans' Administration. He revitalized American foreign policy silencing dictators and strengthening alliances. He moved the US Embassy to the Israeli capitol in Jerusalem. He ended wars and brought soldiers home. He brought jobs and manufacturing back to America. He made the country energy independent. He lowered trade barriers and ended the foreign exploitation of American workers. He told China to stop stealing intellectual property from Americans. He told NATO members to pay their fair share. And he made Communist China come to the table to negotiate a fair-trade agreement.

He did all of this against a background of constant resistance and rebellion by the Democrats who never accepted the 2016 election results and the legitimate transfer of power. Democrats in Congress and the federal government made one coup attempt after another to overthrow the Trump administration. The deep state, the Media, Hollywood, Big Tech, Wallstreet and the Congress united to bring down the President in a lawless display of raw power.

The Democrats were assisted by Communist China that was determined to destroy Donald J. Trump, who had embarrassed them by making public their theft of intellectual property and their unfair trade practices. The Chinese Communist Party declared People's War on the USA. They waged economic warfare, PSYOPS using disinformation and propaganda, electronic warfare and biological warfare (Worldwide distribution of COVID 19.) to attack the USA. And they meddled in the 2020 election to defeat Donald J. Trump.

The biological warfare attack was devastating. It came in the form of the COVID 19 virus Pandemic that ruined the economy, closed schools, shut down businesses and took the lives of countless Americans. The combined attacks directed by the Chinese Communist Party on America resulted in a disaster many times worse than the Japanese attack on Pearl Harbor on 7 December 1941.

Killing the Savior

Given the Chinese Communist interference and the covert efforts to subvert honest elections by the Democrats, the American electorate was never allowed to determine the outcome of the 2020 election. Following the precedent set by the Jacobins during the French Revolution, the American socialists, Democrats and student radicals took matters into their own hands stealing the election in a massive coup. The election was stolen by Democrat controlled state administrations and courts, who unlawfully changed the law to permit massive voter fraud to determine the outcome of the election. Radical political operatives at the precinct level altered the vote count by illegally inserting millions of bogus ballots for Joe Biden into ballot boxes in Pennsylvania, Wisconsin, Michigan, Arizona, and Georgia.

The bogus ballots were made possible by revised laws which opened the flood gates to voter fraud. The revised laws were clearly unconstitutional. State officials, radical courts and democrat governors facilitated the rigged elections by ignoring the Constitution that grants sole authority to determine state voting law to the state legislators. Democrat officials broke their own laws to permit voter identification and verification requirements to be ignored. Requirements limiting the use of absentee voting were abolished. The period for accepting ballots was extended. Ballot harvesting, an unscrupulous invitation to voter fraud, was allowed.

The revolutionary mob in America prevailed. Law and order had been cast aside to allow the radicals to seize power. The legitimate president was ousted by brute force that eliminated the constitutionally chosen chief executive. The People's choice was hounded from office. It was unprecedented in American history, opening federal government to thugs and political hacks forming a revolutionary government of socialists who resembled Jacobins and Bolsheviks more than American citizens.

Efforts by the GOP to appeal the election results to the courts based upon massive evidence of voter fraud and violation of Constitutional Law were dismissed by the courts. The Supreme Court refused to hear the case on procedural grounds that denied the President a fair hearing. It was an outrageous travesty of justice.

The Chief Justice of the Supreme Court disobeyed his sworn duty by refusing to hear a case of noncompliance with constitutional law. State officials and the courts had overstepped their authority to illegally abolish laws to guard against voter fraud. In so doing the constitutional rights of the people to a fair election were nullified. The rights of the President to due process and legal protection from voter fraud were abrogated. By its refusal to hear the case, the Supreme Court certified the coup that took down the President and all hopes for a legitimate outcome to the election. Chief Justice John Roberts was responsible for high crimes against the Constitution. He must be removed from office and the case for the people and the president must be heard by the High Court.

The New Social Order

Two hundred and forty-four years of governance under the constitutional order of the founders was cast aside by a revolutionary mob unrestrained by the will of the people. The Constitution was trampled in the process. The rule of law was annulled. The dangers confronting the American people were and continue to be unprecedented.

America entered an entirely new era in which the founders' checks and balances are no more. The separation of powers appears to have been violated by a conspiracy involving the Chief Justice, the Speaker of the House, and the Department of Justice to subvert the law and overturn the election. The Constitution was cast aside for a future dependent upon the will of the socialist elite. Accordingly, the Bill of Rights no longer has the force of law. It is the raw power of tyranny never seen by Americans, who have become the captives of the revolutionary mob.

Sixty days into the Biden administration finds the Defense Department hard at work purging the military ranks of conservatives. The Biden regime is preparing the military services for their new role in defense of the socialist revolution. Indoctrination of service members has become the priority. In an opinion piece, Captain Joseph R. John (USN Retired) describes the indoctrination in the following words:

"While Communist China, Marxist Soviet Russia, Communist North Korea, and Iran the World's Largest State

sponsor of Islamic Terrorism are preparing for "Total War" with the US, the Biden Administration is destroying the "Combat Effectiveness" and "Unit Cohesion" of the US Armed Forces by having Obama Screened, Politically Correct, Flag and General Officers go on a witch hunt to root out white conservative males from the US Military."

The "Obama Screened Flag" and General Officers are in the process of brain washing the entire US Armed Forces, including the Cadets and Midshipmen at all 5 Service Academies with the Marxist Black Lives Matter radical racist indoctrination of "Critical Race Theory." It teaches all military personnel that America is inherently a racist nation, that all whites suppress blacks, and so many more outright racist lies."

In closing this Chapter, we acknowledge American democracy, and the constitutional order are being put to the test by a calculated socialist coup that stole the 2020 presidential election. The coup abandoned time-honored American tradition, ignored the Constitution, and eviscerated the rule of law. Some have said it was a point of no return. That Democracy was dead, and the Republic has been lost.

Such judgments are unconstructive. Why? Because they presume all is lost, which abandons the cause of the people. If all is lost, there is no hope to preserve our constitutional Republic.

Admitting failure and assuming the Constitution is lost abrogates our responsibility to preserve the last best hope of man. Bold leadership is critical as Americans seek a way out of a monumental constitutional crisis. Instead of a collapse of GOP opposition, we must seek renewal and bold leadership to lead Americans back to our roots in a reaffirmation of the constitutional order, a restoration of the rule of law, and a rededication to God's law.

The challenge we face is to defend the Constitution, reestablish the sovereignty of the people, and restore one nation under God with liberty and justice for all.

Chapter 16:

DESTRUCTIVE PUBLIC POLICIES

Following World War II, America was called upon to lead the Western Democracies in deterring the export of communism by military force. The shield provided by deterrence has permitted the West to prosper while the armed forces of NATO and SEATO stood guard against aggression. We take just pride in the role the Democracies of the West have played in deterring conflict during the Cold War.

Efforts by the Soviet Union and the People's Republic of China to test the resolve of the West resulted in a series of conflicts that we have studied at some length. The role of American leadership has been critical to the success of Western deterrence strategy as the West defended freedom. Unfortunately, not all leaders were up to the task. In this final Chapter we will examine mistakes made in keeping the peace, as well as some closing reflections.

Tragically some leaders have not measured up. Their bad decisions have been based upon destructive public policies that have had disastrous consequences. Had American leadership been more aware of the consequences of poorly thought-out policy changes, those consequences could have been avoided. We will briefly examine some bad decisions and the unfortunate results of poor judgement or irresponsible decisions.

What are we talking about? We are talking about the American role in the assassination of President Ngo Dinh Diem of South Vietnam who was murdered following US Ambassador Henry Cabot Lodge's directions to the CIA station chief to engineer a coup. We are talking about the hasty decision to abandon Western human intelligence (HUMINT) assets in the Middle East because President Jimmy Carter felt spying was bad form. We are talking about the decision of the US Congress to abandon South Vietnam to brutal communist invaders who carried out a genocidal slaughter that was ignored by the press.

We are talking about the decision of President Obama to abandon our Iraqi allies to their fate at the hands of ruthless enemies. We are talking about President Obama's rules of engagement that denied American soldiers the authority to load their weapons before going into combat, and withholding authority to open fire until fired upon, suicidal rules with pointless loss of combat effectiveness and a dramatic escalation in friendly casualties. We are talking about Secretary of State Hillary Clinton's decision to force regime change in Libya resulting in a bloody conflict, the murder of Moammar Qadhafi and the takeover of the country by al Qaeda, a reversal of fortunes for both American and European interests.

These decisions were made without the consent of the people, or an awareness of the consequences of irresponsible actions that resulted in countless lives lost and enormous harm done to US national interests. There are other bad decisions we could cite, but these examples of bad judgments illustrate the point. Given the spotty history of American leaders since WW II, we need an explanation for why we have managed to make such a mess of things?

In most cases the bad decisions have been to take vindictive actions by newly elected leaders to punish their predecessors in office by sabotaging their accomplishments. In many cases it was Democrats punishing their conservative rivals for successfully defending US national interests and besting our communist adversaries. More specifically it was the sympathy Democrats feel for socialist causes that has created backlash at conservative's policy resulting in destructive public policy. In view of the alternating American administrations, the possibilities for mischief have been daunting. The bad decisions have severely hurt American allies. The prospect of continually changing American leadership from one party to the next cannot inspire confidence among American allies.

How Can We Do Better?

A question that needs to be asked is should there be a more consistent foreign policy that overrides the recurring swing from left to right in our governing administrations? If we look back at the Korean war, we see a policy of discounting threats from North Korea and mainland China by the Democrats, followed by a policy of aggressively defending our allies in Asia by Republican leadership. A similar pattern occurred during the Vietnam war where Democrat failure to produce early success produced public dissatisfaction and rejection of the war, followed by Republican withdrawal.

The Republicans arrived too late to salvage the cause of the Vietnamese people savaged by the Left. The American public had turned against the war following years of negative reporting by a hostile media. The betrayal of America by a left leaning press by sewing disinformation and gaslighting to sway the electorate in their decision to abandon South Vietnam played a major role in scuttling American foreign policy.

Similar problems confronted the US in Iraq that resulted from Iraqi failure to observe UN resolutions on WMD. It was an error on the part of Saddam Hussein that was instrumental in precipitating the US invasion. The WMD were found by US troops, but the American accomplishments were minimized by Democrats who opposed President Bush. The press never acknowledged the capture of the WMD by American troops on the ground creating fake news and a controversy that hurt US national interests.

If we look at other conflicts, e.g., Laos, Cambodia, Nicaragua, Serbia, Afghanistan we see fluctuating policy. One policy to justify the risk to American lives at the onset only to be reversed as we changed leadership. Whereas the Bush administration aggressively attacked al Qaeda and the Taliban in Afghanistan, the Obama administration minimized the US role by defunding the Pentagon, altering the rules of engagement thereby placing American troops at a marked disadvantage in close combat, while releasing terrorist prisoners incarcerated at Guantanamo Bay allowing them to return to the battlefield.

How many American lives have been lost as a result of causes that have been abandoned following a change in administrations? There is no way we can ever capture the costs associated with unwise decisions to overthrow, interfere with, change foreign leadership based on decisions made by whoever is running the show on that day. Here again, the nation would benefit enormously from identification of an enduring national strategy and retaining it over time. Unfortunately, polarized political philosophies of the electorate make the formation of a consensus on an enduring national strategy exceedingly difficult.

The Dangers of Socialism

The new wars confronting America are right here at home beginning with the indoctrination and biased teaching to our children that refuses to teach the ugly truth of history to grow an in-house socialist agenda. Under the influence of indoctrinated socialist radicals, we appear to be moving towards socialism. Socialism is destined to failure. As socialism is destructive public policy that has never worked anywhere, it has no chance to work here in America.

In an article titled, "Why Socialism Always Fails," by Mark J. Perry, the author cites three reasons why Socialism has always failed:

1.   Socialism is the Big Lie of the twentieth century. While it promised prosperity, equality, and security, it delivered poverty, misery, and tyranny. Equality was achieved only in the sense that everyone was equal in his or her misery. Socialism may show early signs of success. But any accomplishments quickly fade as the fundamental deficiencies of central planning emerge.

2. The strength of capitalism can be attributed to an incentive structure based upon the three Ps: (1) prices determined by market forces, (2) a profit-and-loss system of accounting and (3) private property rights. The failure of socialism can be traced to its neglect of these three incentive-enhancing components.

3. By their failure to foster, promote, and nurture the potential of their people through incentive-enhancing institutions, centrally planned economies deprive the human spirit of full development. Socialism fails because it kills and destroys the human spirit—just ask the people leaving Cuba in homemade rafts and boats. Today the people of socialist Venezuela are struggling to survive, where just 15 years ago it was a flagship country with the best healthcare system in the world. Today these wretched people must stand to line for hours just to get food.

We must ask the obvious question: If Socialism hasn't worked anywhere else, why would it work here?

Destructive Public Policy

As Communist China wages People's War against the US and builds world class armed forces backed by a WMD arsenal with modern intercontinental ballistic missiles, the US military is focused on enhancing inclusion and social justice. While no one denies the importance of social justice, these programs do little to build a combat ready military establishment. On the contrary they are the tools used to wage class conflict using critical race theory. They are divisive and destructive to unit integrity and combat readiness.

Their use demonstrates the Democrats are waging class warfare that they consider more important than protecting the country from existential enemy threats. As a professional soldier, I am alarmed by what amounts to neglecting essential defense programs in the name of fostering an internal revolutionary struggle by the socialist leaders who have taken control the government.

If we look at the effectiveness of US security agencies we see, CIA, DOJ, NSA, DOD, DHS, military services, and special operations forces, backed up by local law enforcement. There are marked differences in their employment from one administration to the next. Whereas Republicans invest in standing armed forces dedicated to warfighting as essential to meet treaty obligations and keeping the peace, Democrats see the Department of Defense as a waste of resources that competes with more deserving social programs. Consequently, Democrats pursue popular policies that buy votes but are destructive to the preparedness of the armed services.

Whereas Republicans are more likely to recognize that peace and security are the return on investing in national defense, Democrats are more likely to question defense appropriations as diversions of scarce national resources from social programs. Democrats see the armed services as social engineering opportunities. By dismantling traditional norms and standards, they open doors for women, transgendered individuals, and handicapped persons to enter new career fields in the military. These programs reduce combat effectiveness. They amount to affirmative action programs that reduce standards to advance the disadvantaged and handicapped. They do not contribute to war fighting capabilities of the combat infantryman. From the perspective of the professional soldiers who must wage war in response to a national emergency, they are destructive programs that detract from combat readiness.

All Americans must ask the question why we have failed to recognize the 9/11 attack, or the recent COVID 19 virus attacks, or cyber-attacks coming from China and Russia? Consider the drugs entering our country via Mexico and South American countries. This problem was identified over 50 years ago as a serious problem affecting millions of Americans. We have thousands of highly trained officers with the most sophisticated surveillance equipment. Given the investment, the question is why we have failed to prevent drugs from entering the country?

In fairness to the men and women of the customs and border security agencies, we must recognize the failure of the Democrats to control our borders that greatly complicates the problem posed by illegal drug trafficking. The destructive border security programs of the Democrats must be corrected before we can expect to see a return on our investment in the control of illegal drug trafficking. It is another example of the destructive public policy implemented by the Democratic administration of Joe Biden.

The scandal plagued criminal justice system is destructive public policy at its worst. The DOJ protects Democrat criminals, while prosecuting innocent Republicans with fabricated charges of wrongdoing. Shameless Democrats working in collaboration with the corrupt liberal media are okay with a fixed criminal justice system that protects

Democrats, while subverting justice by weaponizing the courts to destroy the opposition party.

Multiple attempts to carryout coups were directed by Congress, the Attorney General and the FBI Director. It is public knowledge that coup attempts were carried out by senior officials in the FBI and DOJ. Such conduct is beyond criminal. It is destructive public policy that is best described as demonic. It clearly demonstrates the evil character of socialism that has taken possession of the leadership of the Democratic Party. It is party politics played according to Saul Alinsky. It is the same Saul Alinsky who dedicated Rules for Radicals to Lucifer, the first rebel.

Weaponizing the Federal government to spy on political rivals by the Obama Administration was destructive public policy. The founders recognized that the Republic could only survive when administered by people devoted to God's Law. Our constitutional republic was never intended to be administered by professional criminals, who are doing everything in their power to destroy liberty and justice for all. The survival of the Republic is jeopardized by the criminal conduct by our elected officials who institute destructive public policy.

For Americans, the threat posed by the consolidation of power by a socialist government with no restraints posed by the rule of law or respect for the sovereignty of the people is enormous. Only now are we becoming aware of the complete lawlessness of the totalitarian regime that has captured control of our federal government. Mercifully, for the American people the separation of powers created by independent state and local governments provides the means to resist the power of the authoritarian administrative state.

The purge of all opposition is the next step in the consolidation of power by the socialists. The authoritarian dictatorship created by the socialists will soon be flexing its grasp on power by attempting to eliminate the Second Amendment and working to crush political opposition posed by the GOP, the Trump base and the Libertarian Party. That is what the internal purge of the military is all about. American soldiers are being brainwashed to wage war on their neighbors and fellow countrymen in the bid for total control by the radical Left. Critical race theory advocated by Black Lives Matter teaches that white privilege persecutes blacks who are victims of systemic racial hatred. It is the false narrative of their political offensive to brainwash the military in their cultural war against Western Civilization.

In writing this book, from the position of a combat veteran who has served for over forty years in many campaigns with the thousands of men and women defending freedom, I see that America is at a turning point in our position as a world power and as a leader of the free world. Unless we can preserve our independence and move towards a well thought out and consistent foreign policy by neutralizing radical demands for a socialist police state, our resources will continue to be wasted and our national interests will continue to be compromised.

I would like to leave you with one thought, if we do not change or modify our domestic and foreign policies by eliminating destructive public policy and rededication of the people to the Constitution, our republic, and God's Law we can never achieve a national consensus. Without a national consensus with consistent agreed upon objectives that surpass an ever-changing government, we will become a country paying billions for wars we can never win.

EPILOGUE

Liberty Vs. Tyranny addresses the very real impact Progressive reformers have had on Americans and their culture. Our goal has been to understand the impact Progressives have had on our lives, our society, and the republic. Our assessment draws on the contributions of scholars like Dinesh D'Souza, whose works have identified falsified historical accounts and restored the integrity of a much-maligned past. We have examined the works of journalists and historians to see the republic under attack through the eyes of Progressive reformers, as well as the perspective seen by Conservatives defending the Constitution.

We have addressed political parties and their philosophies employing the brilliant analysis of Gertrude Himmelfarb. We have examined the origins of the Progressive liberal philosophy, as well as that of the Conservatives. We have looked at social and political changes that have challenged our republic. In the case of slavery, we have examined events that go back to the earliest days of the English colonies in America.

We have examined events that have shaped the socialist legacy to the modern world. We have looked at the impact of the Vietnam War on society from both sides of the conflict. We have arrived at conclusions that challenge the teachings of Progressive reformers and their reforms (e.g., politically correct rules that bind Americans to an alien social contract). Our survey shows the social contract of the alien nation—the Progressive nation—that cohabits with Conservatives in America and subverts the republic by abusing the educational system. These subversive advocates of socialism teach hatred of America and advocate the overthrow of the government."

The Progressive Assault on America

We looked at the events of the 1960s from several perspectives to capture the essence of the cultural war that raged in our midst. It was a time of testing when progressive reformers renounced American foreign policy and supported enemies—foreign and domestic. Our streets were filled with demonstrations denouncing America for waging an immoral war—a charge shown to be false. The liberal fourth estate reported the Vietnam War as it was seen in Hanoi as opposed to the way the war was seen in Washington and Saigon—a betrayal suggesting that the liberal media no longer accepted the American social contract.

Progressives were exposed as a political movement that advocated socialism and rejected American heritage and political culture. The uprising of Progressive reformers created a breach between and within generations as

Conservatives backed America, while Progressives backed the Socialist Front made up of Hanoi, the National Liberation Front, the People's Army of Vietnam, and the Vietcong.

The legacy of the Vietnam War has been a bitter divide between the two sides. Progressive reforms—based on the French Enlightenment—have clashed with American values and tradition based on the American Enlightenment. Whereas Progressives pursue a socialist vision for America, Conservatives remain defenders of the Constitution.

Today Democrats favor socialist policies, income redistribution, socialized medicine and big government, whereas Republicans favor the traditional American political culture and reject revisionist history. Thus, the split that has occurred during the Vietnam War has exposed enduring and fundamental differences between disciples of the French Enlightenment and those of the American Enlightenment. The differences between the political systems advocated are enormous.

The clash of values became open insurrection. The summer of 2020 saw insurrections of rioters attacking police, destroying property, and defying local authorities from New York to LA and from Portland to Atlanta. With the capture of the White House and both houses of Congress, the Left has scored major victories. Legislation passed by Congress accelerates the transition from a free market economy to a socialist state. Given progressive dominance in the liberal media and social media the GOP finds itself in a precarious position.

Nevertheless, the GOP base remains united and in control of many state legislatures. The people remain undecided as demonstrated by the seventy-four million voters who cast their votes for Donald J. Trump in the presidential election. The fact that the GOP base considers the election outcome to have been the result of fraud does not bode well for the peace and tranquility of the country.

Given the Progressive history of intimidation, fabrication, and the use of violence to impose their will, the possibility of a level playing field is remote. It is a contest between amoral Progressives bound by no law except political expediency and Conservative American citizens seeking God's will through ethical and responsible actions. It is an asymmetrical contest that makes the concept of a level playing field meaningless.

Those of us serving in uniform under the American flag during the cultural war have seen our colors burned by our opponents, as well as by those we have fought to defend. We have seen the fourth estate support those we have fought in battle. We have seen the enemies of the USA supported by radical professors of the academic community. We have been betrayed by those we have fought to defend. Nonetheless, men and women in uniform have done their duty despite the infidelity of the Progressive movement.

Through it all, our servicemen and women have kept the faith with their fellow Americans. They have been faithful to their oath to support and defend the Constitution. And they have been faithful to the challenge JFK presented in his inaugural address when my generation has first begun its journey. We have borne any burden in defense of freedom.

I want to express my special thanks to Tony Moore for his support and participation in our publication of Liberty vs. Tyranny. Tony joined our work in exposing the radical political transformation of our times that threatens the Free World and Western Civilization. Educated in the UK, Tony brings with him a sophisticated appreciation of the challenges we face as seen by our European allies. His insights have served to broaden our appreciation of the questions we face as well as providing historical expertise that elucidates threats as seen from the perspective of our European allies. Without Tony's contributions *Liberty Vs. Tyranny* could not have been published.

The conclusions reached in Liberty Vs Tyranny are the fruit of the work of the many soldiers, scholars, and students who have shared our journey. I am most grateful for the many whose generous support has made this work possible, especially Prof. Peter Christian Lutz, Lt. Gen. Thomas Mc.Inerney, Maj. Gen. George S. Patton, and Col. Harry Summers. Their direction and encouragement have made an appreciation of the extraordinary events of our times possible. I also wish to thank my lovely wife, Lynn, whose support has made it possible for an elderly disabled veteran to share with you his views on our turbulent times.

ABOUT THE AUTHOR

Colonel O'Meara served as a cavalryman, infantryman and tankerman in troop units in Europe, Vietnam and the United States. His command experience includes troop duty from platoon to brigade level, as well as his service as the Assistant Division Commander (ADC) for Support of the 24th Infantry Division. His combat experiences included two tours in line units as a lieutenant, captain as a Maj. Gen. with the 1st Cavalry Regiment (ARVN) and the 11th Armored Cavalry Regiment (US). He was decorated five times for valor during his service in Vietnam. He also became Major General George S. Patton's Intelligence Officer during the Vietnam war.

O'Meara studied in Europe earning certification as a Western European Area Expert. He graduated from the Army War College, earning two graduate degrees over the course of his career. He served in the War Plans Division of the Operations Directorate in the Pentagon and as a speech writer in the Office of the Army Chief of Staff. He directed the training development of the M-1 Abrams Tank. He also served as the President of the Army Training Board and as the Senior Army Instructor at the National War College, where he retired from military service.

Following his retirement from the Army, he served as a government contractor for the Army in the Middle East. During his work for the Army in Saudi Arabia, the Army Mission was targeted by al Qaeda in the War on Terror. He was working in the Army Mission Headquarters in Riyadh when a truck bomb that inflicted three hundred casualties on Saudi nationals and Americans destroyed the building.

Colonel O'Meara's published works include *Infrastructure and the Marxist Power Seizure, Accidental Warrior, Only the Dead Came Home, Opening the American Mind, Reflections,* and *Revisiting Revisionist History.* He acted as co-editor and author of *Leadership: Combat Leaders and Lessons.* In addition, he has published numerous articles that have appeared in newspapers and professional journals.

<u>EDUCATION</u>

Civilian

US Military Academy, West Point, NY, BS Civil Engineering, 1959.

University of Wisconsin, Milwaukee Campus, MS Political Science, 1968.

Military

US Army Command and General Staff College, Ft. Leavenworth, KS, MMAS Degree, 1970.

Army War College, Carlisle Barracks, PA, Diploma, 1978.

National War College, Ft. McNair, Washington, D.C., Diploma, 1989.

Awards

Silver Star Medal, Defense Superior Service Medal, Legion of Merit (3 awards), Distinguished Flying Cross, Bronze Star Medal for Valor (2 awards), Bronze Star Medal for Meritorious Service (2 awards), Purple Heart, Meritorious Service Medal, RVN Gallantry Cross (2 awards), Combat

Infantryman's Badge, as well as airborne and ranger qualifications.

Military Service

Thirty years of commissioned service as an armor officer from 3 June 1959 until 1 July 1989. Highest rank held: Colonel. Military specialties: 12, 54, and 28.

COL. O'MEARA - PRIMARY ASSIGNMENTS

Manager Airwork Vinnell (AWV) 1999 – 2000 *Seeb Air Port, Sultanate of Oman*

Served as the Training Manager to establish Quality Management training programs conforming to ISO 9001 standards of excellence. Served as Humans Resources Manager to establish comprehensive Human Resources Management Programs in compliance with ISO 9001 standards of excellence.

Manager, Institutional Training Division, 1995 -1999 *Vinnell, Arabia, Saudi Arabian National Guard Modernization Program (SANG-MP) Riyadh, Saudi Arabia*

Responsible for the training and support of the Staff and Faculty of the National Guard Military Schools. Acted as the advisor to the Commander of the Schools. Responsible for the development, operation and maintenance of Saudi Arabian National Guard ranges, battle simulations, simulators, training devices, training literature, and technical publications. Responsible for the SANG-MP English Language Training Program and supervision of the staff and faculty of the English Language Institute.

Managed a Division of 218 personnel to accomplish the program objectives.

Manager Military Staff 1994 – 1995 *(Riyadh Saudi Arabia)*
Training Branch, Vinnell Corp. Saudi National Guard Modernization Program

Served as the primary contractor responsible for the training of the Headquarters of the Saudi Arabian National Guard, which directed a full-time Bedouin army consisting of over 100,000 personnel. Provided overall direction and supervision of thirty contractor personnel. Responsible for concepts, design and development of the programs, policy and training of the Saudi Arabian Nation Guard.

Manager Vinnell Corp. 1992-1993 *Saudi Arabian National Guard Modernization Program Dammam, Saudi Arabia*

Served as the primary contractor representative in the Eastern Region of Saudi Arabia for support of the National Guard. Provided supervision and direction to thirty contractor personnel for advice and training of the Provincial Staff and Commanders. Provided quality of life and basic needs of contractor personnel.

Senior Advisor, Vinnell Corp. 1991-1992 *Saudi Arabian National Guard Modernization Program, Riyadh, Saudi Arabia*

Planned, developed and presented Force Integration instruction for the Headquarters of the National Guard.

Developed and published the Training Management doctrine for the National Guard.

Senior Army Instructor 1987-1989 *National War College Ft. Leslie J. McNair, Washington, D.C.*

Served as the principal advisor and evaluator of fifty Army officers attending the National War College. Taught military strategy, nuclear strategy, and the operational level of war. Developed and taught an elective: Strategy and the Military Professional.

Assistant Divisional Commander 1985-1987 *24th Infantry Division, Fort Stewart, GA*

Supervised the conduct of maintenance, supply, food service, and medical support for an Army division consisting of 14,000 personnel. Supervised industrial support operations for the Army National Guard and Army Reserve with a budget of $500 million. Supervised the changeover to the M-1 Tank and the turn-in of the M-60 series vehicles. This program included the train-up on the new equipment.

President Army Training Board Command 1983-1985 *Fort Eustis, VA*

Responsible for Army doctrine for training and training development. Developed Army training management doctrine and training literature.

Brigade Commander First Brigade 1980-1983 *Fort Knox, KY*

Commanded a six-battalion brigade numbering 5500 personnel. Responsible for initial entry training of 36,000 tankers and cavalrymen over a three-year period. Directed the training development effort for the M-1 Tank.

Editor Office of Army Chief 1979-1980 Staff Weekly Summary, *HQ, Department of the Army, Washington, D.C.*

Served as the principal speechwriter for the Army Vice Chief of Staff and the Director of the Army Staff. Served also as the editor of the Chief of Staff Weekly Summary, a digest of activities and significant events occurring at the Headquarters Department of the Army.

Battalion Commander Armored Division 1975-1977 *Fort Hood, TX*